The Girls in 509

A COMEDY IN TWO ACTS

by Howard Teichmann

SAMUEL FRENCH, INC.
25 WEST 45TH STREET   NEW YORK 10036
7623 SUNSET BOULEVARD   HOLLYWOOD 90046
LONDON   *TORONTO*

THE GIRLS IN 509

STORY OF THE PLAY

"The Girls in 509" is a comedy for Republicans, Democrats, Independents—in fact, for any voter who wants to
laugh. When a not-now fashionable hotel in New York is
being remodelled, a pair of hermit ladies are discovered
in one of the back suites. They have been there ever
since that black night in November 1932, when Herbert
Hoover lost the election. Deliberately cutting themselves
off from the outside world, they have vowed to remain
secluded until That Man is out of the White House and
a Republican is elected. Led by a professor of journalism
from a small Mid-Western college who is under the impression he is working for the New York Times, the press
descends upon the two ladies. Close on the heels of the
press is the National Chairman of the Republican Party.
Another visitor is the National Chairman of the Democratic Party. As members of one of the country's oldest
and once richest families, the two ladies defy both politicians and are faced with eviction and disgrace. They
retain their independence and privacy, however, when
unheard of wealth pours down upon them, and they move
in the glittering, be-jeweled triumph of the past, to a new
hermitage in the Waldorf-Astoria. "Uniformly bright."
N. Y. Times. "Funny and loony." *N. Y. Daily News.*

To

TURNER CATLEDGE,

gentleman journalist,
who nightly played his role faultlessly, whose
behavior before, during, and after each performance was exemplary—whose good humour
and graciousness are deeply appreciated.

The Girls in 509 was presented by Alfred de Liagre, Jr., at the Belasco Theatre, N. Y., Oct. 15, 1958; direction by Bretaigne Windust; setting and lighting by Donald Oenslager; costumes by Lucinda Ballard.

CAST OF CHARACTERS

(In order of appearance)

MIMSY	*Imogene Coca*
AUNT HETTIE	*Peggy Wood*
OLD JIM...........................	*Fred Stewart*
RYAN, of the Daily News...............	*Les Damon*
PUSEY	*King Donovan*
MISS FREUD	*Laurinda Barrett*
WINTHROP ALLEN	*Robert Emhardt*
SUMMERS, of the Herald Tribune........	*Will Hussung*
JOHNSON, of the Daily Mirror..........	*William Bush*
ROSENTHAL, of the Post	*Sam Schwartz*
FRANCIS X. NELLA.................	*Robert Emhardt*
AUBREY MCKITTRIDGE..............	*James Millhollin*

SCENES

The entire action of the play occurs in the sitting room of a suite, and in the hallway of a not-now fashionable hotel in New York City. The time is the present.

ACT ONE

SCENE 1: *Noon. April 2nd.*

SCENE 2: *A few minutes later.*

ACT TWO

SCENE 1: *One minute later.*

SCENE 2: *Morning. April 3rd.*

SCENE 3: *Evening.*

6

PRODUCTION NOTES

As "The Girls in 509" is a political satire and is, therefore, somewhat subject to the light whims and fancies of time and personalities, permission is hereby granted to future producers and/or directors to bring up to date those few lines which, from moment to moment, may require such assistance.

Two words should be said here with regard to the zebra trap. Come to think of it, two paragraphs might be better. There being no such device in the vocabulary of safari, I might just as well admit that a zebra trap is a device of my own invention, thus saving the property man hours of anguish and ill temper. As presented on Broadway, the zebra trap was an elaborate net which was concealed in the ceiling of the set. When the designated actors stepped onto a kind of sewer cover which was ostentatiously rolled into place on the floor and covered with a small hooked rug, a klaxon horn sounded loudly off stage. The net would then drop, surrounding the actor, a drawstring would tighten the bottom of the net, and the actor would be hoisted to the ceiling.

Less elaborate methods have since been employed successfully to produce the desired effect. A reasonably large, reasonably shallow bowl, equipped to look like an electric light fixture may be attached to the ceiling. In it, neatly arranged, is a fish net. When the "trap" is sprung, the bowl swings open on hinges, the net falls clear, enveloping the helpless actor. Whether one end of the net remains attached to the ceiling or whether it is arranged so that the entire contraption descends upon the actor is left to the discretion and ingenuity of those in charge. It is to be hoped that the rapidly sounding klaxon and the sewer cover on the floor will be retained.

A final paragraph must be devoted to "curtains." Generally, the descent of the zebra trap at the conclusion of Act One, Scene One and Act One, Scene Two evokes such laughter that it is pointless to delay the curtain for the remaining few lines. The lines are there in case the laughter is not great enough. If, however, a whopping chunk of good, solid, clean, healthy, unpledged laughter greets the actors with the fall of the zebra trap, the stage manager is urged to "ring down" immediately. Such moments are too rare to miss.

HOWARD TEICHMANN

The Girls in 509

ACT ONE

SCENE 1

SCENE: *Sitting room of a suite in an old-fashioned hotel in New York City. Furniture is neat but well-used: pictures of Republican presidents abound. The back wall is covered with a tapestry not quite completed. Other evidences of hobbies and collections are sprinkled about. However, this display takes up but three-quarters of the stage. What remains is an area outside the room: a section of hallway, a potted palm, a frosted glass elevator door.*

AT RISE: *Although it is morning, the LIGHTS are still on. Somewhere an ALARM CLOCK rings. A WOMAN'S VOICE is heard from Offstage.*

A WOMAN'S VOICE. (*Off.*) Aunt Hettie? (*Another VOICE makes a sound. The ALARM CLOCK is stilled.*) Aunt Hettie? (AUNT HETTIE *yawns.*) Good morning, Aunt Hettie.

AUNT HETTIE'S VOICE. (*Off.*) Good heavens. Is it noon already?

A WOMAN'S VOICE. Yes. Getting up?

AUNT HETTIE'S VOICE. I don't know, Mimsy. I'm not sure I can face it today.

MIMSY'S VOICE. (*Brightly.*) Well, I am. (*There is the sing-song of setting up exercises.*) One—and—two—and —two—and—one—and—down—and—up—and—up— and—down—and—in—and—out—and—in—and—high —and—low—and—low—and—high—and—touch—your toes—and—

9

AUNT HETTIE'S VOICE. Oh, for mercy's sake, Mimsy, stop that damn exercising and close the window!

(*A WINDOW is closed, Off.*)

MIMSY'S VOICE. I think I'll order now, Aunt Hettie, if it's all right with you. (*Putting on a robe over her nightgown*, MIMSY *enters. She could not have won a beauty contest at 18. Today, she is definitely out of the running.*) Oh, dear, I left the lights on again last night.

AUNT HETTIE'S VOICE. Well, in these times, that's a sin, Mimsy. In these days every penny counts.

MIMSY. We don't pay the electric bill, Aunt Hettie. The hotel does.

AUNT HETTIE'S VOICE. Bother the hotel! A dollar's a dollar! You're beginning to sound like a New Dealer, Mimsy. (AUNT HETTIE *enters. She is an aristocrat with a twinkle in her eye.*) What's breakfast?

MIMSY. (*Picks up the phone.*) Good morning, James. This is 509. Fine, thank you. And you?— Oh, I'm glad. We'd appreciate our breakfast now, James, if it's all right with you.

AUNT HETTIE. Of course, it's all right with him. Tell him we'll have the usual.

MIMSY. We'll have the usual, James.

AUNT HETTIE. (*She is now at a chart on the door.*) Temperature?

MIMSY. James? What's the temperature outside now? — Thank you. (*Hangs up.*) Sixty-eight.

AUNT HETTIE. (*Marking the chart.*) My. This is the warmest April Second since 1939.

MIMSY. Really, Aunt Hettie? Oh, that's wonderful!

AUNT HETTIE. Mimsy. The trap.

MIMSY. Oh. (*Like a busy, busy beaver, with great rapidity and efficiency she drops to her hands and knees in front of the steel hole and looks in.*) Spring coil— ready! (*She races up to the sideboard, throws open the cabinet, looks, closes it.*) Alarm system—ready! (*She lugs the steel ring to the hole and puts it in place.*) Contact plate—in position! (*She twists the plate. Runs to switch.*) Electrical contact—made! (*Throws switch.*) It's all set, Aunt Hettie.

AUNT HETTIE. Tha-a-at's a good girl.

MIMSY. (*Half curtsey.*) Thank you, Aunt Hettie.

AUNT HETTIE. Mimsy, these robes are too warm for this time of year. If I ordered the material, would you run them up on the sewing machine?

MIMSY. Satin and lace are rather expensive. (*Hopefully.*) Of course, we could pawn something.

AUNT HETTIE. Mimsy, dear, in the four-hundred-year recorded history of our family, not one Van der Wyck has ever pawned. Poor people pawn.

MIMSY. Well, what have we been doing?

AUNT HETTIE. *We* have been putting things out to loan. We are impoverished, Mimsy, but so long as we have our name and our heritage, and our books and each other, we will not be poor. Now what the hell could we send to the Lefkowitz Loan Company this time?

MIMSY. (*Getting picture from Up Right table.*) There's always William McKinley.

AUNT HETTIE. I will not part with the president who vetoed the personal income tax law.

MIMSY. Oh, I didn't mean to pawn Mr. McKinley. I just meant the frame. It's sterling.

AUNT HETTIE. Taking him out of his frame would be like taking off his clothes. You wouldn't want to see William McKinley naked, would you?

MIMSY. (*A look at the picture. Then:*) No! (*Replaces picture.*)

AUNT HETTIE. Come, child. Let's dress.

(*They exit into the bedroom. In the corridor, ELEVA-TOR LIGHT is seen rising through frosted glass. Door opens. RYAN, a reporter, carrying a camera, emerges. He begins to photograph the door to 509. A tea cart with breakfast dishes on it emerges. It is pushed by an elderly bellboy. This is OLD JIM, and he is clearly disturbed.*)

OLD JIM. Hold your fire, there, young fella! Pictures weren't part of the bargain.

RYAN. I'm just shooting the door.

OLD JIM. I guaranteed to bring you up here and show you where they live. But that's all. Say, where's that fella come up in the car with us?

RYAN. I dunno.

OLD JIM. For a reporter, he's the most bashful horse in the barn. (*Calling.*) Say. Say, mister? This is the fifth floor. You can come out now.

A MAN'S VOICE. (*From elevator.*) I can? (PUSEY *emerges. He doesn't look like a reporter at all.*) Thank you. Is that their door? (*Crosses Up to door.*)

RYAN. Yeah! What'd *you* give him to get up here?

PUSEY. Nothing.

RYAN. Nothing?

OLD JIM. He just looked sad. Like a parrot I owned when I was a boy.

RYAN. Did your parrot talk?

OLD JIM. Not much. He was from New England.

RYAN. Any animals in 509?

OLD JIM. Not that I know of.

PUSEY. That's quite an interesting piece of news. Would you mind if I made a note of it?

RYAN. What'd you say your name was?

PUSEY. Pusey. That was quite a scoop you had this morning.

RYAN. Quite a what?

PUSEY. Scoop?

RYAN. Where did you say you were from?

PUSEY. I just came from the New York Times. 229 West 43rd Street, New York 36, New York.

RYAN. Scoop, eh? Well, tear out the front page. Hildy Johnson is back.

PUSEY. You *are* the Arthur Ryan who wrote the article in this morning's New York Daily News about the two Smith sisters who are reputed to be hidden away in there?

RYAN. So the Times has decided this is news fit to print? Well. I kind of expected the Mirror here today, maybe the Journal and the Telegram, too, but the New York Times—

OLD JIM. Mr. Ryan, that's quite a story you did.

RYAN. What'd the girls think of it?

OLD JIM. Can't say. They don't read newspapers.

RYAN. Why not?

OLD JIM. Can't say. Haven't delivered one to 'em since 1940. They don't take phone calls, either.

RYAN. Why not?

OLD JIM. They've got the phone bell disconnected, I imagine.

PUSEY. (*Writing furiously in notebook.*) Not so fast, please. I don't want to get any of this wrong. You see, Mr. Ryan, much as I admired your article, there *were* one or two statements which were not substantiated by fact. And as Hyde's textbook on Basic Reporting states, "Facts, facts, facts are what an alert readership demands of a story."

RYAN. Listen, the Times may have the facts. The News has got the circulation.

PUSEY. Now, if you didn't interview the sisters personally, how do you know their name is Smith?

RYAN. He told me.

OLD JIM. It says so on their monthly bill.

PUSEY. How do you know they're Republicans?

OLD JIM. They scream when you say Democrat.

PUSEY. And they are actually recluses?

OLD JIM. They've never come out since I've been here. Nineteen years.

RYAN. Who cleans up their rooms?

OLD JIM. They never let anyone in. I leave fresh linen out here once a week, they take care of the rest.

RYAN. What about repairs? Painting, radiator leaks?

OLD JIM. Hasn't been any decoration in that suite since they arrived. As for the rest, nothing ever seems to go wrong in there. Now, that's all, gents. Got to deliver their breakfast.

RYAN. (*Holds up $5.00 bill to* OLD JIM.) How about getting me inside for some pictures?

OLD JIM. Oh, I couldn't do that. Those are fine women. I like 'em. They're my friends. Besides, I can't see a thing when I go in. It's all dark except for some lights shining into my face, and I never take more'n three steps once I get inside the room.

RYAN. Why not?

OLD JIM. They warned me not to. Ask me, I think the place is rigged with booby traps. Want some pictures of me while I wheel in the cart?

RYAN. Yeah, all right.

OLD JIM. (*Takes bill. He wheels cart to door.*) Aim that camera from over there. This is my good side. (*Knocks, calls.*) 'Morning! It's Old Jim. (MIMSY *appears briefly at the door of bedroom. She quickly draws the drapes, switches off LIGHTS in sitting room, a SPOTLIGHT in the room framed on doorway flashes on, a BUZZER is heard. The door opens, and* OLD JIM *wheels in the breakfast. Takes three steps into room.*) Morning, ma'am. Breakfast.

MIMSY. Thank you very much, James.

OLD JIM. Yes, ma'am. 'Morning. (*And he obediently backs up three steps, closes the door and is back in the corridor.* MIMSY *turns on sitting room LIGHTS. LIGHTS over door go off. Opens drapes. During this,* RYAN *has been shooting flash bulbs with great rapidity. As for* PUSEY, *during the excitement, he faded away.*) There you are. Got enough?

RYAN. Uh huh.

OLD JIM. Let's go down then. Say, where's the man from the Times?

RYAN. I don't know. He must've walked down. Now, my editor wants to make sure no one else is living here.

OLD JIM. They're all that's left. Ladies' beauty parlor on the second floor moved out last week. Sorry to see it go. (*Into elevator.* RYAN *follows.*) What I learned from that place will keep me a single man forever. Do you know that women can be artificial from their toe nails clear up to the hair on their heads? Yes, sir! Everything artificial. Everything!

(*Elevator door closes. Car goes down.* MIMSY *enters, dressed for the day. If the length of her skirt is not quite up to the latest fashion, forgive her. She is reading a book as she crosses room. She automatically pulls in tea cart. By having the cart the exact height as the table, and by tacking the table cloth to a thin wooden board,* MIMSY *is able to pull the cloth, the silver, the dishes, the glasses, everything from the cart onto the table in a single sweep.*)

MIMSY. (*Sits Center of table.*) Aunt Hettie! Breakfast.

AUNT HETTIE. Coming, dear. (AUNT HETTIE, *also dressed for the day; also reading a book, enters.*) I can't decide which of us is the greater ass, Balzac for writing this book, or me for reading it for the eighth time. This heroine of his not only has a one track mind, there's only one word on the track.

MIMSY. What's the word?

AUNT HETTIE. Oh, Mimsy dear, I'm *so* glad you're a good girl.

MIMSY. So am I, Aunt Hettie.

AUNT HETTIE. Promise me you'll always be good?

MIMSY. Well, I'm not sure.

AUNT HETTIE. Mimsy! What's wrong, dear? Your liver bile again?

MIMSY. No, it's just that I don't see why we have to eat oatmeal every morning.

AUNT HETTIE. (*Recovering.*) Oh. Well, Chester A. Arthur ate oatmeal every morning and in his day there wasn't even a *hint* of a corporation tax.

MIMSY. Eating oatmeal won't get rid of the corporation tax.

AUNT HETTIE. No, but *some* one has to keep up *some* of the traditions of the Republican Party, or all we'll have left is anarchy! Eat up, girl.

MIMSY. Damn.

AUNT HETTIE. Mimsy, you will not use profanity.

MIMSY. You swear.

AUNT HETTIE. At my age I'm entitled to something.

MIMSY. What about me? What am I entitled to?

AUNT HETTIE. What would you like that you don't have?

MIMSY. A blow-torch.

AUNT HETTIE. You've got one.

MIMSY. A new one. Do you suppose we could afford that, Aunt Hettie?

AUNT HETTIE. With those lunatics in Washington we're lucky we can afford breakfast, let alone a blow-torch.

MIMSY. (*Taking a spoonful.*) James isn't preparing this oatmeal. He got it from the drug store again.

AUNT HETTIE. How can you tell?

MIMSY. I can taste bicarbonate of soda through and through.

AUNT HETTIE. Well, I like it. All those years of hotel food. At least this is different. Bad—but different.

(PUSEY *raises his hand to knock at door, is too timid, disappears down hallway.*)

MIMSY. You're certain we can't afford a new blow-torch?

AUNT HETTIE. Now, Mimsy, we've been through this before. We've spent enough money on trifles over the years. Correspondence School courses, lessons for you, arts, crafts, hobbies . . . model automobiles, zebra traps, and singing lessons by mail—

MIMSY. But a blow-torch is what I need, Aunt Hettie. What if that radiator opens up in the bedroom again?

AUNT HETTIE. Mimsy, you're old enough to face the truth. One has no reason to be embarrassed when one says one can't afford this or can't afford that. The entire country's doing it. Look at this hotel. Empty.

MIMSY. You think that's still because of the Depression?

AUNT HETTIE. No doubt of it, child. People simply

cannot afford this way of life any longer. Forty-two dollars a month for two rooms. Outrageous!

MIMSY. You're right, Aunt Hettie. We have to watch every penny.

AUNT HETTIE. (*Lowers her book. Touches* MIMSY's *hand.*) Oh, you don't know how it hurts me to hear you say that.

MIMSY. But it's true, isn't it?

AUNT HETTIE. It's true, unfortunately, but . . . (*Shakes her head sadly.*)

MIMSY. Yes, Aunt Hettie?

AUNT HETTIE. Nothing. I was just thinking of the good old days.

MIMSY. Let me tell it this time. When you went out in the evening, you always dressed.

AUNT HETTIE. Oh, the beautiful clothes we wore! Furs and dinner gowns and—

MIMSY. —the gentlemen wore opera capes and silk hats.

AUNT HETTIE. I wish those days were back again, just so I could give all of those things to *you*, Mimsy. Midnight suppers after the opera. And breakfast at six before the hunt.

MIMSY. (*Lost in her own thoughts.*) What do men wear to breakfast, Aunt Hettie? What did my father wear?

AUNT HETTIE. A blue serge suit.

MIMSY. Why?

AUNT HETTIE. *His* father wore one.

MIMSY. (*Crosses back to chair, sits.*) Did all the men in our family wear blue serge?

AUNT HETTIE. Certainly not, dear. Some of them, the early ones, used to wear lace at their throats and cuffs, and sterling buckles on their shoes.

MIMSY. Oh, I wouldn't mind sterling buckles on *my* shoes, but I wouldn't want a man, *my* man, to wear them. I'd like him to wear—boots, perhaps.

AUNT HETTIE. Your father wore boots, English riding

boots. But only when we were up at the place on the Tappan Zee—for the shooting in the fall.

MIMSY. I wonder what it would be like having a man in boots at the breakfast table, Aunt Hettie. Not my father, I mean—a husband. He'd probably smoke. (*Grandly.*) I don't know that I'd allow smoking at my breakfast table. "Please stop smoking," I'd say. (*Raps cup with spoon.*) "Did you hear me? Ugh! Be good enough to stop smoking at my breakfast table."

AUNT HETTIE. (*Her head still buried in her book.*) Send him out to the stables.

MIMSY. (*Directing her attention to her imaginary husband.*) "I will thank you, to enjoy your cigar in the stables."

AUNT HETTIE. Did he go?

MIMSY. He put it out.

AUNT HETTIE. That's very good, dear. One must be firm with the men.

MIMSY. (*Directing her attention to her imaginary husband.*) "And please put down your newspaper— Do you hear me? I shall not tolerate it another instant!— How dare you say that about my aunt!"

AUNT HETTIE. Don't quarrel, children.

MIMSY. "This is the last straw." Aunt Hettie, I'm going to consult my lawyers.

AUNT HETTIE. (*Lowers book.*) Now Mimsy, in our family we do not divorce! Now go back and make the best of it.

MIMSY. I won't.

AUNT HETTIE. (*Snaps book shut.*) Then pretend he wasn't reading the goddamn newspaper!

MIMSY. (*Sensibly.*) All right, Aunt Hettie. If you'd like it that way. (*Sweetly to her unseen husband.*) "Would you care for more coffee, dear?"

AUNT HETTIE. (*Back in the book. Absently.*) No, thank you, dear.

MIMSY. (*Crestfallen.*) There, you see, it doesn't work. I don't suppose I'll *ever* catch one.

AUNT HETTIE. Catch what, Mimsy?

MIMSY. A man.

AUNT HETTIE. Oh, I'm sure you will, Mimsy.

(PUSEY *comes out*.)

MIMSY. How? How, Aunt Hettie?

(PUSEY *approaches the door*.)

AUNT HETTIE. You'll see. (*Rises*.) Come, child, it's time we made the beds and you must get on with your practising.

MIMSY. On top of oatmeal?

AUNT HETTIE. Stand up. Do your vocalizing.

(MIMSY *stands, folds her hands in front of her, assumes a concert-like position and begins to vocalize an aria such as the Jewel Song from "Faust," the Bell Song from "Lakme," or if she can manage the mezzo role, the Habanera from "Carmen."* AUNT HETTIE *beats time, and after a few bars is so carried away that she joins* MIMSY *in singing.* PUSEY, *at the door, is bug-eyed by what he hears. At length, however, he manages to knock.* BOTH GIRLS *break off*.)

MIMSY. (*After a pause, in a whisper*.) That didn't sound like James' knock, did it?

AUNT HETTIE. (*Also a whisper*.) No.

MIMSY. What should we do?

AUNT HETTIE. Don't move.

(*The elevator LIGHT appears.* PUSEY *sees it. He hurries off. Elevator door opens.* OLD JIM *emerges, a letter in hand. He knocks at their door and calls*.)

OLD JIM. It's Old Jim!

AUNT HETTIE. (*Nods reassuringly to* MIMSY.) Yes, James?

OLD JIM. Got a letter for you. If you won't take it, I've got to read it to you. It's from the management.

AUNT HETTIE. We do not wish to hear it, James.

OLD JIM. They write here they've given you ample notice to move. That's true. And they can't remodel the place until you are out.

AUNT HETTIE. We're satisfied with the hotel as it is.

(Elevator BUZZER sounds.)

OLD JIM. I've told you it isn't going to be a hotel any more. As soon as you ladies leave, the reconverting starts and within ninety days in moves the you-know-what.

MIMSY. *(Nervously.)* You'd better stop talking, if it's all right with you, James.

AUNT HETTIE. Who did you say was moving in?

OLD JIM. You know who. A woman's club.

AUNT HETTIE. Yes, but what kind of women?

OLD JIM. *(Reluctantly.)* National Association of Democratic Women.

AUNT HETTIE. No!

MIMSY. Now, Aunt Hettie—

OLD JIM. So what's the earliest day you can leave?

AUNT HETTIE. Doomsday, goddamn it!

OLD JIM. Now, Miss Smith—

AUNT HETTIE. You tell your management the Democrats have done enough! They've taxed me, regimented me, handcuffed my investments, ruined my servants, overpaid the working classes, undercut the constitution, and now they want to throw us out of the two little rooms we have had for 26 years! Well, sir! You tell your employers that the Democratic Party has pushed me about long enough! Here I am, and here I remain!

OLD JIM. Well, ladies, you've got *your* rights. But on the other hand the landlord has got *his* rights, too.

(From the stairwell in the hallway appears a mannishly tailored, immensely efficient, and not at all unattractive young woman. She is angry.)

YOUNG WOMAN. One moment! What right do you have to discuss rights?

OLD JIM. How's that again?

YOUNG WOMAN. Who are you? What's your name, your position here, your immediate superior, your working hours and duties, seniority, if any, and social security number?

OLD JIM. How come you want to know all about me?

MISS FREUD. My name is Freud.

OLD JIM. That explains it.

MISS FREUD. I am not related to the doctor, I am not a doctor, I am not a psychoanalyst, I am not interested in psychoanalysis, I am merely an employee of the Welfare Department of the City of New York who was born with a particularly unfortunate last name. (*Sits bench Right.*)

OLD JIM. You're out of breath.

MISS FREUD. Those stairs. I rang. No answer. You're the first employee I've seen. Where's the desk clerk?

OLD JIM. Right here, ma'am. Also the elevator operator and the bellboy.

MISS FREUD. What kind of service do the guests in this hotel receive?

OLD JIM. Fanciest there is. One employee to every two guests. Even the Queen Mary can't give you *that* kind of luxury.

MISS FREUD. (*Crosses Up to door.*) Now, about your two guests. A story in the Daily News this morning created a good deal of interest in our office. Where are the Smith sisters? I wish to see them.

OLD JIM. Oh, no one ever sees them.

MISS FREUD. There's hardly any point in my conducting an interview if I'm unable to talk to the subjects.

OLD JIM. (*Follows.*) Oh, you're talking to them right now. They're on the other side of that door. Been listening to every word we said. Isn't that right, ladies?

(AUNT HETTIE *nudges* MIMSY.)

MIMSY. That's right, James.

MISS FREUD. How do I know there are two of them?

AUNT HETTIE. There are two of us, young woman.

MISS FREUD. Splendid. (*Projecting*.) Ladies, your Welfare Department understands—unofficially—that punitive measures are about to be taken against you by your landlord. This question is—of course—routine, but are you aware of such measures?

OLD JIM. I've got the registered letter. It just came.

MISS FREUD. Give it to them.

OLD JIM. Oh no, except for correspondence school courses, I never give 'em mail. But I'll tell 'em about it. Ladies—

AUNT HETTIE. Yes, James?

OLD JIM. Beginning noon tomorrow, all services in this hotel are going to be stopped.

MISS FREUD. Be specific. *List* the services.

OLD JIM. After twelve o'clock tomorrow you aren't going to get any heat. You're not going to get any electricity or water, either.

MISS FREUD. That's enough! Attention, ladies! Do you hear me? This is Miss Freud speaking. Do you hear me?

MIMSY. We hear you, Miss Freud. We hear you. Over and out.

AUNT HETTIE. Mimsy!

MIMSY. Well, she does sound like a radio operator, and that course I subscribed to—

MISS FREUD. Do you understand what is about to be done to you? Well, don't worry. Your New York City Welfare Department is standing by.

MIMSY. Really?

MISS FREUD. Your city courts will protect you.

MIMSY. That's nice.

MISS FREUD. Your city government is on the job! And I am ready to prove it.

AUNT HETTIE. Will you bring us a pitcher of water when the tap runs dry?

MISS FREUD. I will go before Judge Samuel J. Litwieler this afternoon and demand an injunction against your landlord. I will secure a writ of mandamus.

AUNT HETTIE. Yes, but what happens when we get thirsty?

MISS FREUD. Madame, that is not the point.

MIMSY. It is, if you don't have any water.

MISS FREUD. Water is not in our department. It's in Gas, Electricity, Marine and Aviation. But I'll do my best.

(AUNT HETTIE *places dish on cart.*)

OLD JIM. I shouldn't bring it up, ma'am, but this building is being taken over by the National Association of Democratic Women.

MISS FREUD. (*Abashed.*) Oh.

OLD JIM. I thought that would make a difference.

MISS FREUD. (*Into the fray!*) We in the Department are above politics.

OLD JIM. You're sure?

MISS FREUD. I am a civil servant. I am not dependent upon the pressures of any political party. I, I am proud to say, have my Social Security to fall back on, my F.O.A.B. pension, my Blue Cross, Blue Shield, State Retirement Fund, City Benefit Plan, and Employees Benevolent Association.

OLD JIM. You don't happen to have a rich husband, too?

MISS FREUD. What can a man give you that a government can't?

OLD JIM. (*He looks at her.*) Well— There are books on that subject!

MISS FREUD. Oh! I'd report you, except the forms take too long to fill out! (*Projecting.*) This is Miss Freud again, ladies. I am leaving. (*Crosses to bench Down Right.*)

MIMSY and HETTIE. Goodbye.

AUNT HETTIE. Come along, Mimsy.

MIMSY. They haven't gone yet.

OLD JIM. Going down.

MISS FREUD. I'll walk. I want to re-check your stairwell. I don't think it has the required amount of illumination. And if I fall—

OLD JIM. You've got the Blue Cross, the Blue Shield, and the Benevolent Association all waiting to pick you up.

MISS FREUD. Sometimes I wonder why I took up social work. I *despise* people. (*She exits by stairs.*)

OLD JIM. Ladies—

BOTH. Yes, James.

OLD JIM. I just want you to know how sorry I am they're doing this.

AUNT HETTIE. Thank you. We'll manage, James.

OLD JIM. I don't want you to move any more than *you* do. Well, I'll be getting along. Just call if you need anything. (*Exits Right.*)

MIMSY. We shall.

AUNT HETTIE. Mimsy, we have work before us. We must collect all the pots, pans, vases, everything that can hold water.

MIMSY. (*Collecting items.*) Oh, it's so exciting, Aunt Hettie. There's the umbrella stand and the bath tub, and Grandmother Van der Wyck's crystal punch bowl and this vase—

AUNT HETTIE. (*Crosses to bedroom door.*) That's the spirit, girl! You're a chip off the old block. Just like your father. Every New Year's Eve he used to take an extra flask with him. "Hettie," he'd say, "they may *carry* me out, but they're not going to *dry* me out!"

MIMSY. Daddy— Daddy used to drink a good deal, didn't he?

AUNT HETTIE. If we only had the branch water that went with his bourbon, we could hold out here forever!

(*They exit into bedroom. OLD JIM re-enters, then goes to their door and listens. He speaks softly.*)

OLD JIM. Miss Smith?— Miss Smith, can you hear

me?— That's good. (*He walks to where the hallway makes a right angle, turns, and then calls softly.*) All right, young fella, you can come out of that hiding place now. I mean you from the New York Times. You're hanging around somewhere on this floor.

PUSEY. (*Emerges somewhat sheepishly.*) How did you know?

OLD JIM. I didn't ride you down in the elevator, and I didn't see you come down the stairs. So I figured you were still here. But that's almost *all* I can figure about you. Kind of mysterious, ain't you?

PUSEY. Me?

OLD JIM. You're not from the New York Times.

PUSEY. No. No, I'm not.

OLD JIM. You're not even a reporter.

PUSEY. It's that obvious, is it? People can always tell I'm not a newspaperman. I don't know how, but they can.

OLD JIM. What are you?

PUSEY. A professor at the Missouri Baptist College for Men.

OLD JIM. What do you teach?

PUSEY. Journalism.

OLD JIM. Well, why're you pretending to be a reporter?

PUSEY. I'm not pretending, I'm trying. But it doesn't work. Nothing I ever do works. The only thing I'm good at is failure. You see, Mr.—

OLD JIM. I prefer folks to call me Old Jim. It's not that I'm so old. It just makes me seem more likable. Now, tell me, did you ever do anything about this business of not making good?

PUSEY. I certainly did. For eight years, five days a week, I went to the college clinic to the psychoanalyst.

OLD JIM. Did it help?

PUSEY. My doctor told me it was a very successful analysis. I'm completely adjusted to failure.

OLD JIM. I still don't understand why you're trying to be a reporter.

PUSEY. You see, I give a course in feature writing at the "Jay" school.

OLD JIM. Where?

PUSEY. "Jay" for Journalism. Of course, I've never actually written a feature story that appeared in a newspaper, but that's not important in the educational world.

OLD JIM. No?

PUSEY. It's the theory behind the subject, plus the ability to communicate that counts.

OLD JIM. Then what're you doing here?

PUSEY. I'm only an associate professor, and the Dean would like to see me move up to a full professorship. The usual way, of course, is to write a book.

OLD JIM. Of course.

PUSEY. But so many professors have written books on feature writing that the Dean thought if I wrote a feature—well, that *would* be different.

OLD JIM. Now, Professor, when you told Ryan of the News that you'd just come from the Times—

PUSEY. I was telling the truth. I had come from there. This is spring vacation. Just after I got to town today I went on a guided tour through the plant of the New York Times. And as our group passed the office of the managing editor, I lagged behind the others and found myself having a delightful talk with a Mr. Turner Catledge. A fine man. Very well grounded in almost every aspect of our profession.

OLD JIM. Almost every aspect?

PUSEY. Oh, a bit weak perhaps in the history of journalism in America—that's my other major course. I took the liberty of mentioning to Mr. Catledge Mr. Ryan's little feature in the Daily News. I pointed out that the New York Times had been scooped on a jim-dandy human interest story. And I pointed out there just might conceivably be more to this story than met the eye, and would he mind if I represented his publication on the story. He didn't mind at all. He was just concerned about my getting around New York. He told me not to get lost; I *believe* those were his words. He took me to the door and waved his hand at me, and said something about getting lost, and I said I *wouldn't* get lost and for him not to worry, and he said he wouldn't—obviously, he had confidence in me—and then I closed the door and I was on my own. Well, I tell you, it was exciting walking around the New York Times building.

OLD JIM. Did you go near the drama desk?

PUSEY. What's that?

OLD JIM. That's where the critics are.

PUSEY. No.

OLD JIM. That's a shame. You might have seen them criticizing.

PUSEY. That isn't what they do.

OLD JIM. No?

PUSEY. No, critics write what we call "critiques."

OLD JIM. Oh. Is that what they do?

PUSEY. Yes, but I'm not interested in that. Professor Cooper gives the course in dramatic criticism. (*A faint trace of deprecation.*) Between us, there's not much to the course. Mostly, he teaches them to hate.

OLD JIM. Well, it's a beginning.

PUSEY. In any case, I left the New York Times building, came here and—well, you found me out.

OLD JIM. Maybe I was able to do that because—well, maybe we're a little alike.

PUSEY. You and I?

OLD JIM. Yes. Y'see, I'm not really a bellboy. I'm an actor.

PUSEY. You don't look like an actor.

OLD JIM. I'm a character actor.

PUSEY. You don't even *sound* like an actor.

OLD JIM. I'm not in character.

PUSEY. If you're an actor, what've you been doing here for nineteen years?

OLD JIM. This is only temporary. I'm in between engagements.

PUSEY. I see. Have you been an actor long?

OLD JIM. Since I was a boy. Ever hear of a place called Skowhegan?

PUSEY. No.

OLD JIM. It's in Maine. That's where I come from.

When I was a boy, they'd just started a summer theatre there. My family needed money. In July and August in those days it was either painting scenery at the Skowhegan theatre, or whitewashing the summer people's privies. And since it was cooler backstage than it was in the back yards, I became an actor.

PUSEY. Have you been in many plays?

OLD JIM. Have I? "The Front Page," "The Bandwagon," "Our Town," "Life with Father," "Death of a Salesman." Those are just the hits.

PUSEY. I saw "Death of a Salesman." What was your part?

OLD JIM. Willy Lohman.

PUSEY. I didn't see you in it.

OLD JIM. That's right.

PUSEY. Why not?

OLD JIM. Other fellow was too healthy.

PUSEY. You mean—?

OLD JIM. I was the understudy.

PUSEY. And "Life with Father"?

OLD JIM. Same thing. I never got near the stage. Howard Lindsay took iron tonic before every performance.

PUSEY. Well, I gather you haven't followed your profession in quite a long while.

OLD JIM. To be in a play nowadays, you have to get in on the ground floor.

PUSEY. The director?

OLD JIM. He doesn't mean a thing.

PUSEY. The producer?

OLD JIM. A figure head. No sir, you got to get to the author, and before he has a line written.

PUSEY. I know a playwright. Of course, he's not professional.

OLD JIM. None of 'em are these days. What's his name?

PUSEY. Martin Elliott. We share an apartment in Bachelor's Hall at school. He's the assistant professor of dramatics.

OLD JIM. Never heard of him.

PUSEY. He's written a very fine play.

OLD JIM. Forget it.

PUSEY. Really it is. Some people here in New York have been encouraging him. The "Theatre Guild" they call themselves.

OLD JIM. The Theatre Guild? Have you read this play?

PUSEY. No. I've heard it, though. Martin reads it aloud to me after every re-write.

OLD JIM. Anything in there for a character man?

PUSEY. Any parts, you mean?

OLD JIM. Parts, walk-ons; anything for an old fella like me?

PUSEY. Oh, yes. The setting is an old soldiers' home.

OLD JIM. How many old soldiers? On stage, I mean.

PUSEY. 42.

OLD JIM. 42 old soldiers. One of 'em's *got* to look like me. I could dye my hair white or wig up. Professor, could you get me into that show?

PUSEY. Well, I'd be glad to recommend you.

OLD JIM. Recommendations only get you as far as auditions. What I want is a signed Equity Contract.

PUSEY. Well, I—

OLD JIM. You're close to the author. Six or eight lines for Old Jim— Please? This means everything to me.

PUSEY. I *said* I'd recommend you.

OLD JIM. You're a hard man to deal with. But if it's a trade you want, you've got it. I'm going to give you that full professorship.

PUSEY. You?

OLD JIM. If a story in the New York Times will do it, you're on the front page already. Every feature writer in town would like an interview with the Smith sisters. I'm going to see you get one—exclusive.

PUSEY. Really?

OLD JIM. (*As* PUSEY *starts into elevator.*) I hate my-self for even thinking of this. On the other hand, it's pretty late for a man of my age to make a start on the stage. It's either now or the Actors' Fund Home. Professor, this is the time of day I collect their breakfast dishes. When I knock at the door, opportunity will be knocking for you.

PUSEY. *I'm* to go in instead of *you?* Oh, I couldn't do that.

OLD JIM. (*Pulls him out.*) Remember what the Dean said.

PUSEY. It wouldn't be ethical.

OLD JIM. There isn't *anything* I wouldn't do for us. (*He knocks. Calls.*) It's Old Jim! (*To* PUSEY.) Have you got your pencil?

PUSEY. Please—

OLD JIM. Paper?

(MIMSY *enters from the bedroom. She turns on the LIGHTS over the door, turns off the LIGHTS in the sitting room.*)

PUSEY. I don't know if I should do this.

OLD JIM. You've got to!

PUSEY. Why?

OLD JIM. For 39 years I've been nothing but an understudy!

(MIMSY *pushes buzzer,* OLD JIM *opens door.*)

MIMSY. All right, James. You may come in now. (PUSEY *is panicky.*) I'm waiting.

OLD JIM. (*Shoves* PUSEY *in.*) Go!

(PUSEY *stumbles in.*)

MIMSY. Why—why, you're not—

PUSEY. No. I'm *not.* I'm— (*He takes a few steps into the room. An alarm KLAXON sounds. The ZEBRA TRAP descends.* MIMSY *turns on the LIGHTS and* PROFESSOR PUSEY, *kicking, clawing, gasping, is seen caught in a net, hanging from the ceiling in the Center of the room.*)

MIMSY. Aunt Hettie! Aunt Hettie! Look what I've caught in the zebra trap!

AUNT HETTIE. (*Offstage.*) A zebra?

MIMSY. A man!

AUNT HETTIE. (*Entering.*) How old?

MIMSY. About forty.

AUNT HETTIE. Throw him back! He's too damn young!

CURTAIN

ACT ONE

SCENE 2

SCENE: *The same, a few minutes later.*

AT RISE: PROFESSOR PUSEY *is roped and efficiently tied to a chair. Not only is he immobile, but the gag about his mouth renders him speechless, but not soundless.* AUNT HETTIE *is circling him cautiously, testing the ropes, while* MIMSY *is busy recovering the trap plate with the ring.*

AUNT HETTIE. You're quite positive these knots will hold, Mimsy?

MIMSY. He won't escape unless he's Harry Houdini, and I don't think he is.

AUNT HETTIE. (*Right of him.*) Well, who are you, sir? (PUSEY *rolls his eyes.*)

MIMSY. (*At switch for trap.*) I'll get that gag off of him just as soon as I get the zebra trap all curled up in its nest again.

AUNT HETTIE. You always thought my insisting on such protection was foolishness, didn't you, Mimsy?

MIMSY. (*Looking at* PUSEY *adoringly.*) Oh, no! I

think it's the most wonderful way I've ever heard of to get a man.

AUNT HETTIE. For years that trap waited for an intruder, and finally one arrived. I congratulate you, Mimsy. It worked perfectly.

MIMSY. (*Looks at* PUSEY *again.*) I'd have been heartbroken if it hadn't. (*The trap disappears in ceiling.*) There we are. All ready for the next one! (*Crosses Down Left.*)

AUNT HETTIE. Heaven forbid! Who wants another? I don't even know what we're going to do with *this* one!

MIMSY. Shall I take off his gag so you may question him?

AUNT HETTIE. That won't be necessary, dear. I'm certain he's quite capable of inclining his head for the affirmative, and shaking it for the negative. Am I correct, sir? (PUSEY *nods "yes."*) Thank you. And now, Mimsy, what do you suggest I ask him?

MIMSY. Oh, all sorts of things! Are you married? (PUSEY *shakes his head "no."*) Are you engaged?

(PUSEY *shakes his head "no."*)

AUNT HETTIE. Do you know who we are?

(PUSEY *nods "yes."*)

MIMSY. Are you a Democrat? (PUSEY *shakes his head "no."*) Oh, Aunt Hettie, we can keep him!

AUNT HETTIE. Just as soon as we find out what his intentions are, we're going to get rid of him.

MIMSY. If his intentions are honorable, may we keep him?

AUNT HETTIE. Certainly not.

MIMSY. (*Crosses to door Right.*) Well, he can't go, Aunt Hettie. I just won't allow it.

AUNT HETTIE. Mimsy, I'm shocked.

MIMSY. I've never been this close to a man.

AUNT HETTIE. Nonsense. Of course you have.

MIMSY. Only when I was a little girl. And when they hold you on their knees and squeeze you when you're a little girl, it doesn't count.

AUNT HETTIE. But darling, what would we do with him?

MIMSY. You could talk to him. He's the first new listener you've had since we locked ourselves in here.

AUNT HETTIE. True, true.

MIMSY. He doesn't know a single one of your stories. You could tell him about the family and how we go all the way back, and about all the Republican presidents and how they helped the people, and how the goddamn Democrats took it away from us and—

AUNT HETTIE. Mustn't swear, Mimsy.

MIMSY. After all, I know your stories so well that sometimes *I* tell them to *you*.

AUNT HETTIE. What would *you* do with him, dear?

MIMSY. Oh, I'd *look* at him. I'd sit and stare at him for hours. (PUSEY *groans*.) He's so beautiful.

AUNT HETTIE. He is?

MIMSY. Oh, I think he's much more beautiful than Charles Buddy Rogers. (*To* PUSEY.) Have you ever seen Charles Buddy Rogers? He was in the last picture I saw before the election. He's my favorite. (*To* AUNT HETTIE.) Oh, Aunt Hettie, we must keep him. Please?

AUNT HETTIE. Well, doesn't *he* have anything to say about it, dear?

MIMSY. No! Finders, keepers.

AUNT HETTIE. How long would you want to keep him?

MIMSY. (*Crosses Up back of him.*) Days, weeks, months, forever!

AUNT HETTIE. Mimsy, dear, I've never seen you like this in my life. What's come over you?

MIMSY. (*Crosses to her.*) I feel so strange, Aunt Hettie. I don't know why. I only know that we mustn't ever let him out of our sight. Oh, please, Aunt Hettie? My birthday is next month. This is what I want most.

AUNT HETTIE. Well, for a few hours perhaps—

MIMSY. Oh, Aunt Hettie, you're so kind.

AUNT HETTIE. (PUSEY *makes noise through his gag.*) Hush. You heard me, sir; hush! I don't recall inviting you, but now that you are in our home— (PUSEY *tries to talk again.*) Mimsy, we simply cannot discuss this man's future before his very eyes. It's rude. He's listening, even if he's not saying anything, and I distinctly dislike being eavesdropped upon. We shall go into the bedroom. (*Crossing below table, Up to door.*)

MIMSY. (*Follows.*) Yes, Aunt Hettie. Oh, now I know where he can sleep.

AUNT HETTIE. Don't be absurd. He isn't going to spend the night here.

MIMSY. But Aunt Hettie, you promised I could keep him.

AUNT HETTIE. Be sensible, Mimsy. How are you going to keep him if he doesn't want to stay?

MIMSY. Do you remember that course I took, the pharmaceutical course I wrote away for in 1939?

AUNT HETTIE. Yes.

MIMSY. Well, I was thinking about morphine.

AUNT HETTIE. Mimsy!

(*They exit. A moment later the elevator comes up, the door opens, and out steps* OLD JIM *with a carpet sweeper and begins gaily to sweep hall. He quickly dusts phone, continues to push carpet sweeper briskly while humming a tune. His mounting gaiety is demonstrated by broader and broader strokes of the sweeper. One of them strikes the door. It opens.*)

OLD JIM. (*Peering in.*) So—this is what it's like in here. (*He sees* PUSEY.) Howdy! (PUSEY *grunts.*) Say! You don't think *I* had anything to do with this? I'm your friend. I'll get you out right now.

(AUNT HETTIE *and* MIMSY *enter from bedroom.*)

MIMSY. (*Blocking his way.*) James, don't you dare touch that man. He's mine!

AUNT HETTIE. (*Crosses Down Left.*) How did you get in here?

OLD JIM. So—this is what they look like. Door was open.

AUNT HETTIE. Lock it, Mimsy.

MIMSY. All right. (*She circumvents the trap plate and closes the door.*)

AUNT HETTIE. The door was ajar, so you came in? James, I take a very dim view of this treachery.

OLD JIM. Yes ma'am, Miss Smith, so do I. I sent this young fella in here with the best of intentions.

MIMSY. Oh, James, thank you. (*She slams bolt on door.*)

OLD JIM. Of course, I knew you mightn't like it, but I didn't think you'd treat him *this* way. I'm going to take him out.

MIMSY. You can't.

OLD JIM. Ladies aren't *allowed* to have strange men in hotel rooms.

MIMSY. Oh, he isn't a stranger.

OLD JIM. He isn't? What's his name? Where's he from? What's he want? (*Pause.*) There you are.

MIMSY. Well, if you know so much, what *is* his name?

OLD JIM. Professor Pusey.

MIMSY. Professor Pusey. Oh, that's a beautiful name.

AUNT HETTIE. A ridiculous name. You've invented it.

OLD JIM. Is your name Professor Pusey, Professor Pusey? (PUSEY *grunts "yes."*)

AUNT HETTIE. And what, supposedly, does he wish from us?

OLD JIM. A story for a newspaper.

AUNT HETTIE. Get him out. Get him out at once! No, Mimsy, not a word. This is the first time in a quarter of a century that our privacy has been invaded. To intrude upon it any further for an article in a newspaper is unthinkable.

OLD JIM. Oh, that's been done already. The News carried a story about you two this morning.

AUNT HETTIE. The Daily News? What did it say?

OLD JIM. Just that there were two sisters name of Smith who were stayin' on here after everyone had cleared out, about how you kept to yourselves mostly.

AUNT HETTIE. There you are, Mimsy. I told you they'd find us sooner or later. I *knew* there'd be no escape.

OLD JIM. My God, they're criminals.

AUNT HETTIE. Don't be absurd. (*Gently to* MIMSY.) Mimsy— Is that why you're sad? Because they've found us?

MIMSY. (*At window.*) No.

AUNT HETTIE. There's another reason?

MIMSY. (*Tightly.*) Yes.

AUNT HETTIE. Because this young man wishes to leave? (MIMSY *turns away*.) And at breakfast I said I wished I could give you some of the happiness that's coming to you, didn't I?

MIMSY. That's all right, Aunt Hettie. We can't force him to stay.

AUNT HETTIE. No, but we can make it worth his while. James, you said this gentleman wanted a story?

OLD JIM. For the New York Times.

AUNT HETTIE. The Times. Oh, yes. I rather like the Times. It's always been a good, solid, dignified, on-the-fence newspaper, doesn't say much, but uses good English. (*To* PUSEY. *Sits chair Left of table.*) Sir, if I were to offer information for a newspaper article, would you give my niece and me the pleasure of taking tea with us this afternoon? My niece pours beautifully.

OLD JIM. Your niece? I always thought, Miss Smith, that you were sisters.

AUNT HETTIE. Well, we're not. And you might just as well stop calling us Smith. That is not our family name. We simply used Smith when we registered here. We didn't wish to be bothered. (*To* PUSEY.) Sir, does the name Van der Wyck mean anything to you?

OLD JIM. Van der Wyck?

AUNT HETTIE. Van der Wyck Park, Van der Wyck Place, the Van der Wyck Building, Lake Van der Wyck,

Van der Wyck, New York. Though we're not too proud of *that* community. It's gone Democratic in every election since 1912.

OLD JIM. Van der Wyck. You're a Van der Wyck? A real Van der Wyck?

AUNT HETTIE. I am.

OLD JIM. You're not kidding, are you?

AUNT HETTIE. (*Pulling herself up to her full height.*) Do I look it?

OLD JIM. (*Pause.*) No, Miss Van der Wyck.

AUNT HETTIE. Thank you, James. You know, Mimsy, it's rather pleasing to hear oneself called by one's own name after all these years.

OLD JIM. But there aren't supposed to *be* any Van der Wycks any more.

AUNT HETTIE. We—are the last of the Van der Wycks. Some years ago, Rensselaer, the last surviving *male* member of the family, fell from a window of his triplex apartment overlooking Park Avenue. Three months later, his sister, Henrietta, dropped out of sight.

OLD JIM. From the same window?

AUNT HETTIE. I am Henrietta. And this is Rensselaer's daughter.

OLD JIM. I remember now. There was a big to-do about your disappearance. Oh, *very* big. On a par, I'd say, with Judge Crater. Say, maybe he's around here somewhere.

AUNT HETTIE. Oh, Mimsy, we haven't given Mr. Pusey a chance to accept our kind invitation. (*She gestures for the gag to be removed.* MIMSY *does so.* PUSEY *moistens lips, swallows. He is agitated.*)

MIMSY. Will you stay?

PUSEY. Van der Wyck! Your ancestors must have known Peter Stuyvesant.

AUNT HETTIE. Know him? They appointed him!

PUSEY. I'll stay! In my History of American Journalism 109 Course I devote an entire lecture to one of your forebears, Henrick. He defended Peter Zenger in America's first libel action. He was a fine lawyer.

MIMSY. He was a fine lawyer, and a big crook.

(*Elevator BUZZER, insistently.*)

AUNT HETTIE. Mimsy, dear, untie our guest. Keeping a man roped to a chair isn't the hospitality for which our family is remembered.

(*Elevator BUZZER.*)

OLD JIM. (*As* AUNT HETTIE *starts to usher him out.*) Lots of action in the lobby. They probably want to come up here. But don't you worry, Professor. I'll keep 'em downstairs long enough for you to get that story.

AUNT HETTIE. And James, since this has been about the busiest morning we've had in the last 25 years, should anyone else wish to see us—we're out.

OLD JIM. You haven't left the room in 25 years, but you're out? Yes, ma'am. (*He closes elevator door and goes down.* AUNT HETTIE *closes door to 509 and returns to the sitting room.*)

MIMSY. He's ready, Aunt Hettie.

PUSEY. (*Presenting pencil and notebook.*) This interview won't take long at all. As Franklin said—

AUNT HETTIE. (*Crossing, Left, she freezes.*) Franklin who?!

PUSEY. Benjamin Franklin.

AUNT HETTIE. (*Continues Left.*) Oh.

MIMSY. Professor Pusey, we've agreed never to mention That Man's name again.

PUSEY. What man?

AUNT HETTIE. Your 32nd President of the United States. Let me tell you about That Man, sir!

MIMSY. (*Quickly.*) Professor Pusey, the interview—if you don't mind.

PUSEY. Oh, no, not at all. That's what I'm here for. Now— (*He almost places chair on trap plate, corrects himself in time.* AUNT HETTIE *has taken a cigarette, lighted it, and placed it in white holder. She is now smoking it. Seated in her chair Left of table. It is tilted at that familiar angle.* PUSEY *does a take.*)

AUNT HETTIE. Yes, I know what you're thinking. But That Man copied this from me.

PUSEY. Now, these questions, Miss Van der Wyck, will fall into two categories. "A," your family, "B," how you and your niece happened to lose yourselves from the world and become such a mystery.

AUNT HETTIE. (*Laughing.*) Gracious, we're not a mystery. And we didn't lose ourselves. We've known where we were all the time. Why, we haven't budged from here since the night we checked in.

PUSEY. And when was that?

AUNT HETTIE. November 5th, 1932. The night of Herbert Hoover's re-election, Mimsy and I went to Mr. Hoover's Victory Ball, only he wasn't re-elected and the Victory Ball was like a wake. You've never seen so many unhappy millionaires in your life.

PUSEY. (*To* MIMSY.) You wouldn't object, Miss Van der Wyck, if I asked *you* a question?

MIMSY. Oh, no, Professor! I'll do anything.

AUNT HETTIE. Mimsy!

MIMSY. That is, I'll *say* anything.

AUNT HETTIE. Mimsy!

MIMSY. What would you like to know, Professor?

PUSEY. In 1932 you must have been a young lady.

AUNT HETTIE. She still *is!*

PUSEY. A very young child?

AUNT HETTIE. That's better. You may answer him now, Mimsy.

MIMSY. Yes, I was very young then.

PUSEY. What were you doing at Mr. Hoover's Headquarters?

MIMSY. I was being honored. After Mr. Hoover was to have made his Victory speech, I was to hand him a dozen roses.

AUNT HETTIE. They wilted quite early in the evening.

MIMSY. Just after Kansas went into the Democratic column.

AUNT HETTIE. We left after that.

MIMSY. We came straight here. We didn't even go home.

PUSEY. Why not?

AUNT HETTIE. During the 1932 Election I was Treasurer of the Republican Campaign Chest. I didn't *ask* for the post, needless to say. But *all* of those gentlemen— (*A proud move toward the pictures on the wall.*)—every Republican President since the Grand Old Party was founded, had a Van der Wyck heading up the Election Campaign Chest.

PUSEY. And so they chose you?

AUNT HETTIE. They chose my brother, Rensselaer.

PUSEY. I thought he jumped?

AUNT HETTIE. He did. Right in the middle of the campaign. And after Rensselaer was gone, Mr. Hoover said he wouldn't have anyone except a Van der Wyck for his treasurer, so—

PUSEY. Was it difficult in those days raising money for Mr. Hoover?

AUNT HETTIE. That was why poor Rensselaer jumped.

PUSEY. How did *you* do?

AUNT HETTIE. Oh, extremely well! I didn't solicit funds from the men, of course. I didn't know anything about politics. I simply had their wives to a series of luncheons. Their wives didn't know anything about politics either, but that was the only way we could get the money for Mr. Hoover. I gave my word to each of the ladies that our candidate would certainly be elected, and when he wasn't—well, I don't know how Mr. Hoover felt that night, but I was giving a dinner party at our home for 150 of my largest contributors, and when he lost, I was too humiliated to face a soul!

PUSEY. How could you be so certain? Didn't you even suspect he might lose?

AUNT HETTIE. Obviously, sir, you do not read the Literary Digest.

PUSEY. No, not any more, Miss Van der Wyck. (*Back to pencil and notes.*) So from Republican Headquarters you came here to ride out the storm. How is it you never went home?

AUNT HETTIE. I did not choose to face people to whom I had broken my word. And Mimsy—being the dear child she is—loves me as much as I love her, so together we wait for the revival of the Republican Party.

PUSEY. Miss Van der Wyck, they say you don't read papers, but haven't you had *any* news since 1932?

AUNT HETTIE. Of course, we have.

MIMSY. (*Crossing to window.*) We used to be able to lean out this window and watch the news bulletins go around the Times Building, but in 1940 they put up a billboard. What does it mean "Peps-eye-Cola"?

AUNT HETTIE. (*Rises.*) And besides, after the 1940 election, I didn't *want* to get any more news. That finished democracy in the United States of America.

PUSEY. Why?

AUNT HETTIE. The Daily News said if That Man got in again, it would be the end of free elections in this country, and he *did!*

MIMSY. Aunt Hettie, please!

AUNT HETTIE. (*Crosses Down Left.*) I tell you, sir, That Man in Washington is a traitor to his class! He's a—

PUSEY. What man?

MIMSY. Franklin Damnation Roosevelt.

AUNT HETTIE. (*Paces Down Left to Center to Down Right.*) And don't defend him in *my* presence, sir! I know all about That Man! We were born in the Hudson River Valley within five miles of each other. Our family has looked down on his for generations. We hated those Roosevelts before it was fashionable. It is utterly inconceivable that a man whose family refused to vaccinate its hogs should become President of the United States! (*Sits chair Down Right.*)

PUSEY. Miss Van der Wyck, he isn't President any more.

AUNT HETTIE. (*Long pause.*) What's that?

PUSEY. A Republican is President now.

AUNT HETTIE. A Republican is in?

PUSEY. Oh, yes. I don't know for how long, but he's in.

AUNT HETTIE. A Republican is the *American* President? (*Rises.*)

PUSEY. That's right.

MIMSY. Aunt Hettie.

(AUNT HETTIE *sits in chair Left of table.* MIMSY *and*
PUSEY *also sit.*)

AUNT HETTIE. You're certain of this news?

PUSEY. Oh, yes.

AUNT HETTIE. Positive?

PUSEY. Absolutely.

AUNT HETTIE. When did it happen?

PUSEY. 1952.

AUNT HETTIE. (*Rises.*) 1952. Oh, blessed year!
(*Throwing her arms about* MIMSY.) Mimsy, we're saved.
We're back in the White House. I was right, Mimsy.
Late, but right. What is his name, sir?

PUSEY. I don't think you'd know him.

AUNT HETTIE. Oh, well, it doesn't matter. Glory Hallelujah! We're back in Washington.

MIMSY. Aunt Hettie, you're crying.

AUNT HETTIE. Tears of joy, darling, tears of joy!
Young man, I can't thank you enough. Mimsy, dear. Get
the champagne.

MIMSY. Yes, Aunt Hettie. (*She hurries into the bedroom.*)

AUNT HETTIE. You won't object, sir, to drinking a
toast, even if the wine hasn't been properly chilled?

PUSEY. No, indeed, Miss Van der Wyck.

AUNT HETTIE. (*Crosses Down Left.*) It's such glorious
news.

PUSEY. I'd think it would be, for you.

AUNT HETTIE. For me? Aren't you a registered Republican?

PUSEY. No.

AUNT HETTIE. Sir—!

PUSEY. On the other hand, I'm not a registered Democrat, either.

AUNT HETTIE. (*Sits table.*) Splendid! I can convert you. Sit down. You remind me of what my Godfather, Mark Hanna, once said. He said, "We could keep the Republican Party in Washington forever if we just had enough people like you, simple, unaffected, unpledged damn fools."

MIMSY. (*Enters with tray, glasses, bottle.*) I've opened it, Aunt Hettie, if it's all right with you.

AUNT HETTIE. If it's all right with me? Mimsy dear, this is the happiest moment of my life! (*She pours the champagne.*)

MIMSY. And mine, Aunt Hettie.

AUNT HETTIE. (*Raising her glass.*) I give you our glorious Party, friend of the people, protector of the widowed and orphaned, guardian of our destiny, hope of our future.

MIMSY. The Republican Party!

AUNT HETTIE. The Republican Party! (*They drink. Quickly lower glasses.* AUNT HETTIE, *a half smile.*) Mine tastes a little flat.

MIMSY. Mine, too.

AUNT HETTIE. I can't understand why! Look at the bottle, Mimsy. What year is it?

MIMSY. 1929.

AUNT HETTIE. No wonder!

(*The elevator arrives. Out pour* OLD JIM, RYAN, *a group of* REPORTERS *and* WINTHROP ALLEN. MR. ALLEN *is an elegantly dressed, handsome, middle-aged Arrow-collar man. He is also a slicker. He is trying to talk, but the* REPORTERS *are bombarding* OLD JIM *with questions.* RYAN *heads for the wall phone and dials it. Inside,* AUNT HETTIE, MIMSY *and* PUSEY *listen at the door after extinguishing living room* LIGHTS *and turning on* LIGHT *over the door.*)

SUMMERS. Van der Wyck. Are you sure about this?

OLD JIM. Yep.

JOHNSON. The genuine Van der Wycks?

ROSENTHAL. They're supposed to be dead.

ALLEN. Gentlemen, may I say something?

ROSENTHAL. In a minute, Mr. Allen.

SUMMERS. Listen, Pop, how long have you known them?

ROSENTHAL. How long you gonna be on that phone, Ryan?

RYAN. Hours! (*Into phone.*) City Room, please.

JOHNSON. Are they big tippers?

ROSENTHAL. Isn't there another phone?

ALLEN. Gentlemen, please! I must ask you to let *me* get a word in. After all, I called this press conference. I paid for lunch and the cab fares.

ROSENTHAL. You didn't tell us they were the Van der Wycks.

ALLEN. I didn't know till we walked into the lobby.

SUMMERS. Who do they pay their bills to, Pop?

SUMMERS. How about it, Pop?

ALLEN. Gentlemen, I'm trying to talk.

JOHNSON. Is it by check or cash, Pop?

OLD JIM. Pop?

JOHNSON. What about the Make-It-At-Home cabin cruiser? Where do they keep it?

SUMMERS. How about it, Pop?

OLD JIM. Pop? pop!

ALLEN. My good man. My *dear* chap.

JOHNSON. Look, Mr. Allen, we've gotta get this news.

SUMMERS. You haven't answered my last question.

SCHWARTZ. Mr. Allen, we don't mean any disrespect.

RYAN. No, I think he's gonna blow up.

(*Ad-lib.*)

OLD JIM. Quiet! (*And the ad lib subsides.*) Tell me. What paper are you from?

ALLEN. My dear friend, I am Winthrop Allen, National Chairman of the Republican Party.

RYAN. (*Into phone.*) Hello, Eddie? Ryan.

ALLEN. 509. That's where they live?

OLD JIM. Mind if I ask what you want with the ladies?

RYAN. (*Into phone.*) No, not Smith, Eddie. Van der Wyck.

ALLEN. When I read in this morning's News that these two dear souls have remained in that room for twenty-six years out of fear for the Democrats, I said to my-self—Winthrop Allen, I said, these two little ladies are the champion Republicans of us all!

RYAN. (*Into phone.*) I dunno, Eddie, he's making a speech.

ALLEN. No, Mr. Ryan, that's what I want *them* to do. I am here now to issue an invitation to these two great ladies to allow me to present them to the great Republican Convention in the great city of Chicago in the great month of July.

RYAN. (*Into phone.*) Did you get that, Eddie?

ROSENTHAL. How does he know they're not insane?

ALLEN. (*Crossing to him.*) Who said that? Who made that statement? Who intimated these ladies are insane? It was you, wasn't it? Own up, man.

ROSENTHAL. All right. So I said it.

ALLEN. What paper are you from?

ROSENTHAL. The New York Post.

ALLEN. I should have guessed it! All your boss wants is to have Max Lerner write stories about crazy people.

ROSENTHAL. We give a lot of space to Earl Wilson's mother-in-law, too.

ALLEN. Pay no attention to this idealistic do-gooder, gentlemen.

JOHNSON. (*Seated bench Down Right.*) Rosenthal, an idealist? His mother is a Republican precinct leader.

ALLEN. Really? What district?

ROSENTHAL. 24th A.D. The Bronx.

ALLEN. (*Crossing Left.*) Oh, very good. I'm proud of your mother.

ROSENTHAL. I help her home from the polls.

ALLEN. I'm proud of you, too, my boy.

ROSENTHAL. So what're you going to do with these two dames?

JOHNSON. Yeah. What do you want with 'em in Chicago?

ALLEN. Riding up in this elevator, gentlemen, I realized that the Van der Wyck family has contributed more financial aid to the Party than any other.

OLD JIM. Now you know what he wants with them in Chicago.

ALLEN. On the contrary. I came here thinking their name was Smith. I came here so that the members of the magnificent Republican Party in convention, their magnificent candidates, and the magnificent television audience would have an opportunity to see what true, rock-bound Republicans are. Now, if you'll just come with me, gentlemen, I'll show you what the real grass-roots think. (*He knocks at the door of 509.*)

RYAN. (*Into phone.*) Hang on, Eddie, he's trying to get in.

ALLEN. I trust and hope I am addressing the Misses Van der Wyck? This is Winthrop Allen, National Chairman of the Republican Party.

AUNT HETTIE. (*At door.*) James, is this some more of your treachery?

OLD JIM. No, ma'am.

ALLEN. I knew your brother, Rensselaer. *My* father worked to raise funds with *your* father, Ulysses S. Van der Wyck. And *my* grandfather accepted the largest contribution in the party's history from *your* grandfather, Jean LaFitte Van der Wyck. May I see you?

AUNT HETTIE. Well, your family has been taking it from ours for so long, I'm afraid to let you in.

ALLEN. Madame!

AUNT HETTIE. Well, I warn you, we don't have much left.

ALLEN. (*Crestfallen.*) You don't?

MIMSY. Does that mean we can't come to Los Angeles?

ALLEN. Well, uh—of course, you can. (*He looks around and sees the* REPORTERS.) If you'll just let us in—

AUNT HETTIE. Well, we might let you in, Mr. Allen, but no one else. None of those reporters.

ALLEN. Sorry, boys. I'll be out later. Stick around for a statement. (*To* AUNT HETTIE.) All right, Miss Van der Wyck. Our first meeting will be off the record.

AUNT HETTIE. Very well. Just wait till we unbolt the door.

MIMSY. (*Springs forward to do so.* AUNT HETTIE *restores sitting room LIGHTS, turns off BIRD'S-EYE.*) I'm so excited! My! The Chairman of the Republican Party. Mr. Allen, it's such an honor.

ALLEN. (*To* REPORTERS.) And you boys thought they were crazy. You see? Nothing's wrong with them. They're fine, clear-thinking, American patriots. That's what they are. (*He strides into the room 5 steps and is whisked up to the ceiling in the zebra trap.*)

MIMSY. Aunt Hettie! There's one for you!

ALLEN. Help!

AUNT HETTIE. Oh, dear, this is just like the night we came here. The Republican Party up in the air!

CURTAIN

ACT TWO

Scene 1

Scene: *The same, a minute later.*

At Rise: *The LIGHTS in the corridor outside 509 are at half. The* Reporters *are seated in various positions, waiting. Inside 509,* Aunt Hettie, Mimsy *and* Pusey *are gathered about* Winthrop Allen. Mr. Allen, *safe at last in a chair, is mopping his brow with a handkerchief. Is it reasonable to assume he is shaken?*

Allen. (*Seated Right of table.*) Of course, I understand, Miss Van der Wyck. No hard feelings at all. It could happen to anyone—I suppose.

Aunt Hettie. (*Left of him.*) We were almost as surprised as you. We forgot it was on. We're so unaccustomed to anyone coming in here, that to have that trap go off twice in one day—

(Mimsy *by switch Down Left; watches trap rise.*)

Allen. Twice? You don't think I'm going up in that again?

Aunt Hettie. Goodness, no, Mr. Allen. Professor Pusey preceded you.

Allen. Professor? What Professor? Where is he?

Aunt Hettie. Why, he's right beside you. You're still dizzy, aren't you, Mr. Allen?

Allen. I told you. I have acrophobia. That's a fear of being up high. Pusey? (*Rises.*) How do you do? How did *you* get here?

Pusey. (*Crossing Down from Up Right.*) About the same way as you. I took five steps into the room and the zebra trap brought me the rest of the way.

48

ALLEN. Zebra trap?!

AUNT HETTIE. Surely, Mr. Allen, you can't believe it was deliberate.

ALLEN. I can't believe it's part of the hotel equipment, either.

MIMSY. (*Down Left.*) Oh, it isn't, Mr. Allen. We sent away for the trap ourselves. We saw it advertised in a magazine.

ALLEN. And you just couldn't resist it.

AUNT HETTIE. It was a necessity. We had all of our money here in cash. We had to have some way of protecting it.

ALLEN. What's the matter with the banks?

AUNT HETTIE. (*Sits her chair.*) Why, Mr. Allen, where have you been? Since 1929 banks have been failing at the rate of 164 a day.

ALLEN. But that's all over. They *can't* fail now.

PUSEY. (*Writing in notebook.*) "They do not trust banks." You don't mind if I use that for my article, do you?

MIMSY. No, we don't mind at all. I mean, if it's all right with you, Aunt Hettie. (AUNT HETTIE *smiles and nods.*)

ALLEN. Did you say you were doing an article, Pusey? What paper?

PUSEY. The—

MIMSY. New York Times.

ALLEN. I'm glad you're here, Pusey. I want the Times to be the first to carry a story of this importance. I want New York; no, I want America; make that the Nato nations; yes, *and* the Russians, to learn the story of these ladies' past, and of their future. The past: frightened, intimidated by a political system they know to be bad for themselves and their country, they hide in a storm cellar, cringing, waiting, praying. The future: their prayers are answered, the popular tidal wave of the glorious Republican Party sweeps over everything—bringing sunshine, light, and hope to a grateful America. (PUSEY, *seated Right, taking notes.*) Step one: as soon as the

Van der Wycks learn that the Republican team is in Washington, they joyfully give up their lives of darkness, dampness, and depression—

AUNT HETTIE. Oh, is the depression over?

ALLEN. Uh—yes. We ended it.

AUNT HETTIE. I'm so glad. Does Roger Babson know?

ALLEN. Who?

AUNT HETTIE. Roger Babson. He predicted the Depression.

ALLEN. Let's not be identified with people who don't have faith in America. (*To* PUSEY *again, crossing Up to sideboard Center.*) So as soon as they learned we were in again, Pusey, they gave up being hermits, moved out of this fire trap, and agreed to appear before the great Republican Convention in the great city of Los Angeles. What a story this will make, Pusey! And after the newspapers, I'll call in the newsreels, the magazines, television.

MIMSY. What's television?

ALLEN. Remember movies? Well, television is the same thing and just as bad, only now it's in your house.

MIMSY. Is Charles Buddy Rogers in television?

ALLEN. Almost every night, but very late.

MIMSY. Just imagine! Charles Buddy Rogers right here every night till very late. Aunt Hettie, I don't care if President McKinley *does* go naked, we have to buy a television!

ALLEN. (*Timidly to* AUNT HETTIE.) You don't care if President McKinley—? Is it true that you have a Make-It-At-Home cabin cruiser in the other room?

AUNT HETTIE. Nonsense. It's only a canoe that Mimsy started.

MIMSY. And you can't use it because they didn't send the paddles.

(*Offstage sound of RADIATOR popping.*)

AUNT HETTIE. Mimsy—

MIMSY. Oh, mercy. That's the radiator in the bedroom again.

AUNT HETTIE. Go to it, Mimsy.

MIMSY. (*Crosses to bedroom door, puts on welding gloves.*) I do hope this won't be a welding job. (*She exits.*)

AUNT HETTIE. Mr. Allen, won't you sit down? Now, as for our going to a political convention, I'm very much afraid that's out of the question. My niece and I are quite shy, and I'm sure there are a great many people there. Besides, I'm not at all sure you'd want me there. I might ask questions.

ALLEN. What kind of questions?

AUNT HETTIE. Where do we stand on taxes?

ALLEN. (*He is relieved, sits chair Right of table.*) Oh. Well. That's fine. Taxes? We're against them.

AUNT HETTIE. Splendid.

ALLEN. Miss Van der Wyck, the Republican Party has *always* been against taxes.

AUNT HETTIE. Good. And now that we're in Washington, we've eliminated them?

ALLEN. What was that again?

AUNT HETTIE. Taxes. The Republican Administration has eliminated them?

ALLEN. Well—not all of them.

AUNT HETTIE. But *some* of them?

ALLEN. Uh—yes. I think that's safe to say. We've eliminated *some* of them.

AUNT HETTIE. How gratifying. Which ones?

ALLEN. Which ones would you like to hear about?

AUNT HETTIE. The Income Tax. Is that gone?

ALLEN. What else would you like to hear about?

AUNT HETTIE. It's not gone, then?

ALLEN. (*Rises; paces.*) Well—uh—Miss Van der Wyck, these are unusual times.

AUNT HETTIE. What about the gasoline tax?

ALLEN. And such times call for increased sacrifices.

AUNT HETTIE. The inheritance tax?

ALLEN. We must re-affirm our beliefs.

AUNT HETTIE. Any of the Federal excise taxes?

ALLEN. We must pledge anew our loyalties.

AUNT HETTIE. At least you've repealed the goddamn Social Security Tax?

ALLEN. We must see to it, Miss Van der Wyck, that our over-all superiority and leadership is maintained.

AUNT HETTIE. Leadership in what? Taxes?

ALLEN. Well, uh—

AUNT HETTIE. Tell me, now that *we* are in Washington, what have we done about Federal jobs?

ALLEN. On that score you don't have to worry, Miss Van der Wyck. We cleaned house, top to bottom.

AUNT HETTIE. Good.

ALLEN. We lopped off more useless, overpaid Democrats from the public payroll than you can imagine.

AUNT HETTIE. Down with the office holders!

ALLEN. You'll be pleased to know that good, sound Republicans are holding down those jobs now, (*Sits.*) and we've created a few thousand *new* ones that *they* never even dreamed of.

AUNT HETTIE. But Mr. Allen, we're committed to *reducing* the number of Federal employees.

ALLEN. Where'd you get that idea?

AUNT HETTIE. It's in our platform.

ALLEN. Come, come, Miss Van der Wyck, who remembers a platform?

AUNT HETTIE. (*Rises.*) I do. Mimsy.

MIMSY. (*Off.*) Yes?

AUNT HETTIE. Where's that 1932 platform?

MIMSY. (*Off.*) It's on the second shelf, beside "Crime and Punishment."

ALLEN. You saved that old chestnut?

AUNT HETTIE. I was a member of the committee that wrote it. (*Gets pamphlet from shelf.*) Here we are. Now let me see. (*She opens it.*) Oh, I know what I wanted to ask. Did the Democrats ever go over the limit set for the national debt?

ALLEN. Uh—*they* didn't, but—

AUNT HETTIE. Oh, that was nice of them. And now

that we've balanced the budget, the debt must be going down.

ALLEN. Well, uh—

PUSEY. Miss Van der Wyck, the budget isn't balanced yet.

AUNT HETTIE. Oh, but it must be, Professor. (*Tapping the pamphlet.*) Right here we pledged to the American people that if elected we would balance the budget. Didn't we, Mr. Allen?

ALLEN. Look. Can't we talk about something else?

AUNT HETTIE. Certainly. I'd like to go back to taxes. It says here, "We favor a drastic reduction—"

(PUSEY *rises.*)

ALLEN. Now, let me tell you something, Miss Van der Wyck. Cooped up here, hiding out, you don't know what's going on.

AUNT HETTIE. Oh, I know what's going on, Mr. Allen. What's going on is the same thing as when the Democrats were in. The only things that are different are the names of the politicians. Oh, there's a difference between Republican and Democratic voters, but not between their politicians. Those vultures not only stand for the same principles, they also have the same goals: the first is to get elected and the second is to stay elected.

ALLEN. (*Rises.*) Well, I'm glad I found out about you here and not in Chicago.

PUSEY. That was an excellent statement, Miss Van der Wyck. Would you repeat that last part again so I can be sure my notes are correct?

AUNT HETTIE. In a moment, Professor. I thank you, Mr. Allen, for having opened my eyes. Now would you do me another favor? Accept my resignation from the Republican Party.

ALLEN. With pleasure. The other side is the one that caters to the lunatic fringe.

AUNT HETTIE. And now if you'll be kind enough to remove yourself from my apartment.

ALLEN. Your apartment? You haven't paid rent here for eight months.

AUNT HETTIE. We are waiting for a check, sir.

ALLEN. Your eviction notice is on Judge Madison's calendar. His clerk tells me they won't get around to it for six months. But Fred Madison doesn't forget past favors. If I asked for it, he'd put you out of here within forty-eight hours.

AUNT HETTIE. How dare you do that!

ALLEN. Your friend from the New York Times has been busy making notes on what we've been saying. If he runs that story— Pusey, these ladies don't like moving. They like their privacy, their quiet, their own little world. You think about that, Pusey.

PUSEY. (*Crosses to Center.*) Oh, I wouldn't want to cause these ladies any trouble. Consider the story dropped. (*Hands him notes.*)

ALLEN. (*Starts out.*) That's more like it.

AUNT HETTIE. Mr. Allen?

ALLEN. Well?

AUNT HETTIE. Heaven forgive me, but I think you and your so-called Republicans are Democrats!

(ALLEN *makes a quick exit into foyer. The* PRESS *comes to life.*)

RYAN. Did you see 'em, Mr. Allen?

JOHNSON. How are they?

ALLEN. Out of their minds.

ROSENTHAL. I told you they were crazy!

ALLEN. Out of their ever-loving minds, boys, about the Republican Party.

MIMSY. (*Enters from bedroom. Motions to* PUSEY, AUNT HETTIE.) Come see what I've done. (PUSEY, AUNT HETTIE, MIMSY *exit into bedroom.*)

ROSENTHAL. How about a statement, Mr. Allen?

SUMMERS. You can tell us something now.

ALLEN. Not now.

JOHNSON. What's wrong? Did the girls cool off on the Republican Party?

ALLEN. Who said that? Who asked that question? It was you, the man from the New York Post, wasn't it?

JOHNSON. No, sir. Johnson of the Journal American.

ALLEN. The Journal American? (*Shaking his head.*) I don't know what's happening to poor Bill Hearst. Hiring a man like that.

RYAN. Well, *have* they cooled off on the Republican Party?

ALLEN. Nonsense. They think it's the finest institution on God's green earth. In fact, one of them said to me— here's a statement, boys—one of them with tears in her eyes, mind you, said to me, "God, in his infinite wisdom, must have created the Republican Party." That's touching, isn't it?

ROSENTHAL. It ought to go great in the Bible belt.

ALLEN. That's what *I* was thinking, too.

RYAN. And so you said it.

ALLEN. Who said that! Who made that statement!

(*The elevator arrives.* OLD JIM *opens the door, the* RE-PORTERS *start into the car.*)

JOHNSON. What else went on in there, Mr. Allen?

ROSENTHAL. How about it, Mr. Allen? We need a story.

ALLEN. Very well. Here's your story, boys. I got it from a sweet little lady in there. The average American's opinion of the Republican Party. Do you know what it is?

OLD JIM. (*Holding open the elevator door.*) Going down!

ALLEN. Who said that! Who made that statement!

(*He exits into the elevator. Door closes, LIGHT goes down.* MIMSY *emerges with a wrench which she places on the sideboard, and with the gusto and self-satisfaction which accompany the successful*

*completion of a well-done job, she removes a pair
of heavy work gloves or gauntlets. A smitten and
impressed* PROFESSOR PUSEY *follows her.*)

PUSEY. Soldering a collar onto a radiator neck. That's
the finest job of work I've ever seen.

MIMSY. (*Archly.*) Oh, you have no idea the things I
can do, Professor.

PUSEY. I certainly admire you.

MIMSY. (*Modestly.*) Oh, any red-blooded American
girl could solder a radiator.

PUSEY. Well, it's always nice to have a handywoman
around the house.

MIMSY. And it's handy to have a man around, too.

PUSEY. (*Preening himself.*) Heh, heh. Is it?

MIMSY. My, it surely is.

PUSEY. Well, I suppose living as you do under these
conditions, you rarely, if ever, see a man.

MIMSY. (*Airily.*) Oh, I wouldn't say that.

PUSEY. (*Taken aback.*) You wouldn't?

MIMSY. No, indeed. Every six weeks I used to see a
man. The window cleaner. Of course, there was always a
pane of glass between us.

PUSEY. Do you mind if I ask you something personal?

MIMSY. Oh, no!

PUSEY. I've never heard the name Mimsy before. What
does it mean?

MIMSY. My mother loved flowers. She wanted to name
me after her favorite, "Hydrangea," only my father
wouldn't hear of it. They compromised on Mimosa. Did
you ever hear of anyone called Mimosa before?

PUSEY. No.

MIMSY. Would you rather I'd been called "Hydrangea"?

PUSEY. Oh, no. You look like a perfect Mimsy to me.

AUNT HETTIE. (*Enters from bedroom.*) Oh, I don't
know what to do!

MIMSY. Aunt Hettie, what's the matter?

AUNT HETTIE. (*Crossing Right.*) Well, one minute I'm

ready to take down those Republicans. The next I don't think I should.

MIMSY. Poor Aunt Hettie, leaving the party after all these years—you must be terribly unhappy.

AUNT HETTIE. Well, I am and I'm not.

MIMSY. You're not?

AUNT HETTIE. One doesn't get a chance very often to tell a politician what one thinks of him. They only show their faces at election time. After that, their snouts are so deeply buried in the public treasury that all one can see of them is their backsides. Come to think of it, there isn't much difference.

MIMSY. You said Mr. Allen said we belonged to the lunatic fringe. Wherever did he get *that* idea?

PUSEY. Lunatic fringe was a phrase Teddy Roosevelt first used. He was speaking to the—

AUNT HETTIE. (*Icily.*) Professor Pusey, if you intend to remain in this room long enough to take tea, you simply must not use that word.

PUSEY. But this was *Theodore* Roosevelt. He was a Republican.

AUNT HETTIE. Dammit, he was a Roosevelt first!

MIMSY. (*Steps down to her.*) Aunt Hettie. I will not allow you to speak to Professor Pusey like that.

AUNT HETTIE. Mimsy.

MIMSY. You're always telling me about the family, how courageous and spirited we are.

AUNT HETTIE. And who is to say we aren't?

MIMSY. I am. If you're going to allow Professor Pusey to sacrifice his story just because a big fat Republican threatened us, you're not much of a Van der Wyck!

AUNT HETTIE. Mimsy!

MIMSY. Now you march right up to that telephone and do something about that story.

AUNT HETTIE. Who do you think you are? Me?

MIMSY. I'm a Van der Wyck.

AUNT HETTIE. Quite right. (*She goes up to phone.*) What a shock this is going to give James. (*She picks up phone.*) Hello, James? Please connect me with the New

York Times. It's a newspaper. That's right. I said connect me with them.

MIMSY. I'm so excited. This is the first outside telephone call we've made in twenty-three years.

AUNT HETTIE. Make a note of this, sir. I want you to tell the Times everything. Especially, my leaving the Republican Party. That's another reason why I'm doing this, you know. The Republican Steering Committee. I want my resignation to come to them as a shock. Hello. Is this the New York Times? Give me Mr. Adolph Ochs— He did? Oh, I'm sorry to hear that. Well, who's in charge now?

PUSEY. Mr. Catledge is the one I'd like to speak with.

AUNT HETTIE. Do you have a Catledge in your organization? Very well, I'll speak with him, please.

PUSEY. If you don't mind, Miss Van der Wyck.

AUNT HETTIE. In a moment. Hello. Is this Mr. Catledge? This is Henrietta Kinderhook Van der Wyck— That is *precisely* the name I used—

PUSEY. Miss Van der Wyck.

AUNT HETTIE. Why, I haven't been anywhere except right here.

MIMSY. Aunt Hettie! It's Professor Pusey who wants to make the impression.

AUNT HETTIE. What, Mr. Catledge?— Oh, but you've already *sent* a reporter to see us— Pusey— Mr. Pusey— Oh, yes, there *is* such a person, Mr. Catledge, and he has *such* good manners. My niece and I have asked him to stay for tea. Well, I'll put him on. (*She hands phone to* PUSEY.)

PUSEY. (*Sits Center chair.*) Hello, Mr. Catledge? This is Professor Pusey— Pusey!— I was in your office just this morning. . . . Missouri Baptist College for Men!— Tha-at's right. No, sir. I didn't get lost. Remember that feature story in the News? Well, the ladies aren't named Smith at all. It's Van der Wyck— No, I don't believe any other reporters have seen them— (*To* MIMSY.) Is that true?

MIMSY. That's true, Professor. We haven't seen a single one of them! Only you! Just you.

PUSEY. No, Mr. Catledge, they weren't aware of the elections. Yes, they do. Winthrop Allen told them. Oh, they were delighted, only they've resigned from the Republican Party. You see, they had a copy of an old Republican platform and they expected the Republicans to live up to it. No, Mr. Allen didn't like it at all. My giving you this story means they're going to be dispossessed— They haven't paid it for eight months— Yes, sir, I'll tell them that— They won't talk to anybody else. Just me, Pusey— Pusey!— P-U-S-E-Y— Adam Pusey— Adam.

MIMSY. The first man!

PUSEY. Oh, a by-line would be very nice, Mr. Catledge. Yes, I'll stay. Thank you, sir. (*Hangs up, beaming.*) "By Adam Pusey, Special Correspondent to the New York Times." My! Wait till they see *that* in the Jay School.

AUNT HETTIE. (*Crossing to Down Right chair.*) Damn, damn, damn!

PUSEY. Did I say something wrong?

AUNT HETTIE. To be dispossessed. Think of it! The last of the Van der Wycks put out on the street like— like—

MIMSY. Like the Astors were before Uncle Nicholas brought them that shipment of beaver skins. (*To* PUSEY.) That was in the late seventeen hundreds.

AUNT HETTIE. Yes, and it put a stigma on the Astors, Mimsy. Somehow, they've never quite recovered.

PUSEY. Excuse me, but are you saying you're broke? (*A stony silence.*) Well, you can't be. Mr. Catledge said you're two of the richest women in the United States.

AUNT HETTIE. Poppycock.

PUSEY. Well, he's the managing editor of the New York Times and he ought to know.

AUNT HETTIE. We're the ones who don't have the money, so we ought to know better.

PUSEY. Well, Mr. Catledge can't be *completely* wrong. Where did it go?

AUNT HETTIE. Where does money *always* go? Into other people's pockets.

MIMSY. Since we're so close to you now, Professor, I can tell you the truth. The day after we got here, our butler brought all the cash Aunt Hettie had hidden in her handkerchief drawer, our clothes and her jewels to the hotel. He brought the jewels in a brown paper bag. He told everyone it was a bag full of bagels. Do you know what bagels are, Professor?

PUSEY. No, I don't.

MIMSY. Neither do we. It isn't in the dictionary yet. It must be a slang word for diamonds.

PUSEY. Well, where *are* the diamonds? Couldn't you sell them? I mean, at a time like this—

AUNT HETTIE. We put them out to loan, I'm ashamed to say. It took nine generations of Van der Wyck women to bring that collection together. It took me only twenty-six years to break it up. In twenty-six years there are a great many meals to pay for, tips to the staff, and Christmas presents and loans to chambermaids and old bellboys. When one has had money for so long, one feels a sense of responsibility accompanies it. At least, that's what we were brought up to believe.

PUSEY. Would ninety-one dollars be any help? That's all I've got left. It's very expensive visiting New York.

AUNT HETTIE. No, thank you, Professor.

PUSEY. It doesn't seem possible. The Van der Wycks with no money. I suppose it's been trickling away for generations.

AUNT HETTIE. (*Crossing Left.*) Don't you believe it, sir. My father was so rich they used to say he hired a man just to dust the money.

PUSEY. Then where did it go?

MIMSY. The stock market crash.

AUNT HETTIE. My brother Rensselaer was wiped out.

PUSEY. Everything?

AUNT HETTIE. (*Sits, her chair.*) Yes. Everything—

except a great many debts, a few of his hobbies, and his dear, dear memory.

PUSEY. What were his hobbies? Maybe they're worth something.

AUNT HETTIE. (*A sad smile.*) No, I'm afraid not, Professor. Rensselaer found pleasure in financing inventions, foolish ones. No, don't get your hopes up. (PUSEY *sits chair Center of table.*) At one time or another, Rensselaer held patents on no less than eleven perpetual motion machines. He owned the sole rights to a candle that never burned down.—Only it doesn't work. There are inventions no one can understand, not even the inventors, I'm afraid. Outlandish, ridiculous things. A little window box to cool a room in summertime. What did your father used to call it, dear?

MIMSY. (*Left of her.*) An air conditioner.

AUNT HETTIE. Imagine! An air conditioner.

PUSEY. You own—?

AUNT HETTIE. And then there was a material to take the place of wax paper and eisenglass.

MIMSY. Daddy named it cellophane.

PUSEY. You holds the patents to—!

AUNT HETTIE. And then, one day, he and his school chum, Rene DuPont, bought something that was going to replace silk stockings.

PUSEY. You hold the patents to nylon?

AUNT HETTIE. Unfortunately, we do.

PUSEY. (*Bolts for the phone.*) Hello, Mr. Catledge!— I mean, get me the New York Times!— Mr. Catledge! Hello! Hello! *Somebody*, listen!

CURTAIN

ACT TWO

SCENE 2

SCENE: *The same, early next morning.*

AT RISE: *A wire is clearly seen leading from the tele-*
phone up the wall, across the ceiling, through the
wall to the foyer, across the ceiling of the foyer to
a fire bell on the far wall, over elevator. At the
table, AUNT HETTIE, MIMSY, *and* PUSEY *are break-*
fasting.

MIMSY. (*Center.*) Are you sure you don't want to
read the paper, Professor Pusey?

PUSEY. (*Right.*) No, thank you.

MIMSY. Positive? Go ahead. Read it aloud.

AUNT HETTIE. (*Left. Looking up from her book.*)
Mimsy, dear, we have all read the Times this morning.
It's quite exciting seeing the Professor's article on the
front page.

PUSEY. Thank you.

AUNT HETTIE. But since I read it aloud, and Professor
Pusey read it aloud, and you read it aloud, there is no
need to read it aloud again.

PUSEY. The telephone hasn't rung, yet?

MIMSY. Don't worry. When it rings, you'll hear it.
Professor? Do you have boots?

PUSEY. For snow? I find rubbers are enough.

MIMSY. I mean English riding boots.

PUSEY. I'm allergic to horses.

MIMSY. That's a shame. Do you smoke?

PUSEY. I tried once. It made me dizzy.

MIMSY. Well, if it didn't make you dizzy, would you
smoke at breakfast?

AUNT HETTIE. Mimsy, even if he did, we don't have
stables to send him to any more.

MIMSY. No, but now, if we wanted, we could afford
to buy the stables back again, couldn't we?

AUNT HETTIE. Yes, dear, if what Professor Pusey told us is true.

MIMSY. It wasn't just Professor Pusey. There was Mr. Catledge. He not only said it over the telephone, he printed it.

AUNT HETTIE. Yes.

MIMSY. And then there was that lawyer of ours you called.

AUNT HETTIE. That's when I realized we were rich again, when Rollo McKittridge said he'd cancel a previous appointment to see us. Then, when he said there'd be no need for us to go all the way down to his office in Wall Street, that he'd come here instead, then I knew we were *stinking* rich again! Mimsy, do you still want a new blow-torch?

MIMSY. (*Looking at* PUSEY, *who is Down Right gathering improvised bed made from window seat cushions.*) Not any more, I don't. I want something else now.

AUNT HETTIE. (*Clearing her throat.*) We'll talk about that later, dear.

MIMSY. Let's talk about it now. Professor—?

AUNT HETTIE. Mimsy. Breeding, dear, breeding.

MIMSY. That's just what I'm thinking about.

AUNT HETTIE. Mimsy!

MIMSY. I'm sorry, Aunt Hettie. It's the excitement. Yesterday was new and different and thrilling but to-day—well, I can't begin to *imagine* what today is going to be like.

(*A FIRE BELL sounds. It rings the length of a tele-phone ring and then cuts.*)

AUNT HETTIE. My God, Mimsy, what bell did you hook that damn telephone up to?

(*BELL rings.*)

MIMSY. There's only one bell on the floor. The fire bell. (*It RINGS again.*)

AUNT HETTIE. Turn it off!

MIMSY. You'll be sorry.

(*The FIRE BELL starts, but* MIMSY, *with a pair of pliers, snips the bell wires.*)

MIMSY. There. Now what will James think? I told him he could ring us this morning and now he can't. And I stayed up half the night rigging this circuit to the fire bell. And you and Professor Pusey just sat here and talked about those patents and the family and a lot of help you were.

AUNT HETTIE. You're the one who took the course in electrical engineering, dear. (*To* PUSEY.) The electrical course came just after the course in painting and wallpaper hanging.

PUSEY. (*Picks up phone.*) Excuse me, ladies, but the usual way to get it to stop ringing is to answer it instead of cutting the wires.

AUNT HETTIE. It's been so many years, it didn't occur to us.

MIMSY. Well, now that we've cut the wire to the bell, how can anyone call us?

PUSEY. I noticed at the New York Times, they don't use bells on the telephones.

MIMSY. No?

PUSEY. Lights. A little light goes on instead of a bell.

MIMSY. A little light?

PUSEY. It's quite colorful, too. Red, white, green.

MIMSY. I have just the thing! (*Races to the bedroom door, and out.*)

PUSEY. I'm sorry to put you to all this trouble, Miss Van der Wyck, but, after all, I *am* a journalist now and my editor insists on keeping in touch. (*Beat.*) "My editor."

(MIMSY *enters with Christmas tree lights wrapped around a rolling pin and starts to string them up.*)

AUNT HETTIE. Tell me, Professor, have you never worked on a newspaper before?

PUSEY. Oh, I've worked on them, but not for long. I was fired after the first story from almost every newspaper in the country. There was an exception. The editor of a paper in Boston kept me on for a whole week because he refused to recognize any wrong in me.

AUNT HETTIE. And what paper was that?

PUSEY. The Christian Science Monitor. So you see, I've always been a failure—except yesterday and today, on this one story. And that's why, when Mr. Catledge instructed me to stay close to you two ladies, I asked if I might spend what was left of last night here. (*Picks up window seat cushion.*)

MIMSY. (*The lights are on a string. She attaches them.*) Were you comfortable, Professor?

PUSEY. I've never had a better night's sleep in my life.

MIMSY. Well, you know what they say. If you find a bed that suits you, never leave it.

AUNT HETTIE. Mimsy! (*Christmas tree LIGHTS blink.*) Good God! What's that?

(PUSEY *crosses Down with cushion.*)

MIMSY. The telephone, Aunt Hettie. Someone's calling. (*Into phone.*) Hello?— Yes— Thank you— Uh huh— Uh huh— Fine—That's very kind of you— Now, who is this?— Who?— Who!! Oh dear. Just a minute, please. I'll have to talk this over with Aunt Hettie. (*Almost speechless to* AUNT HETTIE.) A— There is— Aunt Hettie?

AUNT HETTIE. Yes, dear? It's all right. You may speak.

MIMSY. A Mr. Francis X. Nella is downstairs, Aunt Hettie.

AUNT HETTIE. Who is he?

MIMSY. I don't think I should tell you.

AUNT HETTIE. Mimsy.

MIMSY. Very well. But first sit down. (AUNT HETTIE

does.) Professor Pusey, is there water in that glass? (PUSEY *nods.*) Aunt Hettie, Francis X. Nella—

AUNT HETTIE. Yes?

MIMSY. —is National Chairman of the Democratic Party.

AUNT HETTIE. Water!! (PUSEY *hands her glass.*) What does he want?

MIMSY. He told me to tell you that the Parties had changed so much that if Warren G. Harding were alive today, he'd be the senior Senator from Texas.

AUNT HETTIE. Mimsy, invite that gentleman up.

MIMSY. (*In phone.*) Aunt Hettie says to come up. (*She hangs up. LIGHTS blink again immediately.*) This hook-up certainly works, doesn't it? (*She picks up phone.*) Hello? Yes. James— Yes— Yes, it's all right to bring Mr. Nella up, but I don't know about the others. I'll ask her. (*To* AUNT HETTIE.) James says the lobby is filled with reporters and cameramen and people from every charity on the tax deductible list.

AUNT HETTIE. (*Rises, crosses Center.*) Instruct James that we will see no one but our lawyer.

MIMSY. After Mr. Nella, only Mr. McKittridge, James.

AUNT HETTIE. And now, Mimsy dear, do precisely what I ask. First, say goodbye.

MIMSY. (*In phone.*) Goodbye.

AUNT HETTIE. Now hang up. (MIMSY *does so.*) And now rip the damn thing out of the wall! (MIMSY *rips phone cord from wall automatically.*)

PUSEY. Why did you have her do that?

AUNT HETTIE. Those people in the lobby, Professor. All of them want something. And I can just imagine what it is.

PUSEY. Really?

AUNT HETTIE. Money. My great-grandfather had a motto. "If you want to keep your money, lose your friends."

PUSEY. How very sad.

AUNT HETTIE. Yes. Do you know how he wound up? Owning Bethlehem Steel.

MIMSY. (*Crossing to Down Left.*) Aunt Hettie, would
it be all right if I hide? I'm frightened. I've never seen
a Democrat before.

AUNT HETTIE. (*To her.*) Don't be ridiculous, dear.
They're no different than we are. Except underneath.
What did you say the gentleman's name was, Mimsy?

MIMSY. Mr. Francis X. Nella. What do you suppose
he looks like?

AUNT HETTIE. Politicians are like black cats at midnight. You can't tell one from the other.

(*Elevator comes up. Door opens.* OLD JIM *points with
his hand.*)

OLD JIM. Room 509 is to the right, Mr. Nella.

(FRANCIS X. NELLA *emerges. He wears the same clothes
and the same expression as the Republican Chairman. In fact, BOTH CHAIRMEN ARE PLAYED
BY THE SAME ACTOR.*)

NELLA. Thank you, thank you.

(OLD JIM *closes elevator door. LIGHT goes down.*
NELLA *goes to 509. Beaming broadly, he rubs his
hands together and knocks.*)

MIMSY. He's here!

AUNT HETTIE. Answer the door, dear. (*A sudden
thought.*) Mimsy! That goddamn zebra trap!

MIMSY. It's disconnected, Aunt Hettie. (*Projecting.*)
Yes? Who is it, please?

NELLA. Francis X. Nella. (MIMSY *opens door.*) Miss
Van der Wyck?

AUNT HETTIE. Yes?

NELLA. (*Crosses to Right.*) Allow me to congratulate
you on your glorious discovery of the glorious Democratic Party in this glorious city of New York in the
glorious month of April. In spite of past differences you

and I have much in common. Artificially divided by party symbols, in truth we stand together, shoulder to shoulder, back to back, with our eye on the ball, hand in hand, tooth and nail, one country, indivisible, with liberty and justice for all. You can't object to that, can you?

AUNT HETTIE. You left out nip and tuck. May I present my niece, Mimsy, and Professor Pusey.

NELLA. How do you do? Pusey? Pusey? That was a brilliant job of writing you did, Pusey. That story could bring the Times right back into the Democratic camp. You write another couple stories along the same line and there'll be a place for you in the publicity department of our party.

MIMSY. (*To* PUSEY.) A promotion already! That's wonderful, even if it *is* with the wrong side.

NELLA. From now on, it's the right side, Miss Van der Wyck. That's what I'm here to convince you of.

AUNT HETTIE. (*Sits her chair.*) Well, I don't know. I— I'd like to find out where you people stand on certain issues. Sit down, sit down. (NELLA *sits chair Right of table,* MIMSY *chair Down Right,* PUSEY *behind her.*) For instance, when your Party went to Washington in the early thirties, you showed a marked preference for college professors. Present company excluded, of course, are you still close to the academic mind?

NELLA. Miss Van der Wyck, we're behind 'em a hundred per cent.

AUNT HETTIE. You *haven't* changed. You're still for economists who never had to meet a payroll?

NELLA. Oh, *those* professors. They've been out for years. We're behind the new professors.

AUNT HETTIE. May I ask why?

NELLA. We've got to have 'em if we're going to put a man on the moon.

AUNT HETTIE. To the moon? Someone's going to the moon?

NELLA. It is our hope that *we* are.

AUNT HETTIE. Well, let it be *your* hope. I haven't been down to the corner for twenty-six years. Now, may I ask about those wasteful public power projects you began? The TVA, and the Boulder Dam.

NELLA. That's Hoover Dam now. We're against it.

AUNT HETTIE. What about those political machines you had in the big cities? Tammany Hall?

NELLA. We're against it.

AUNT HETTIE. What about the difference of opinion in your Party between the North and the South?

NELLA. We're against it.

AUNT HETTIE. Where do you stand on unemployment?

NELLA. We're against it.

AUNT HETTIE. And daylight saving time.

NELLA. We're against it. Except where they want it.

AUNT HETTIE. And I presume you're against a high tariff?

NELLA. We are.

AUNT HETTIE. But you're against too low a tariff, too?

NELLA. We are.

AUNT HETTIE. Splendid, Mr. Nella. Now, what are you for?

NELLA. We're for getting in again. Miss Van der Wyck, I'm going to be honest with you.

AUNT HETTIE. Up till now you've been lying?

NELLA. If we are going to accomplish those aims so dear to your heart and mine, lower taxes but a bigger army, a smaller national debt but larger schools, less extravagance, but better roads, lower prices but bigger dividends, shorter hours but higher wages—if we are to accomplish that ordinary, everyday run-of-the-mill miracle of the ages, Miss Van der Wyck, we need your help.

AUNT HETTIE. If you think you're going to get me out to a political convention, and parade me about like a side show, I won't do it!

NELLA. Miss Van der Wyck. That isn't what I'm here for at all. You'll never guess what it is I want.

AUNT HETTIE. Money!

NELLA. It'll take money to win the next election, and we are, I am sorry to say, stone broke. But that shouldn't surprise you, Miss Van der Wyck. After all, we are the people's Party.

AUNT HETTIE. Which people?

NELLA. *All* the people.

AUNT HETTIE. Then why don't *they* give you the money?

NELLA. They don't have it. The other people do.

AUNT HETTIE. You expect me to contribute to the Democratic Party?

NELLA. It's your only hope.

AUNT HETTIE. And you really think you'll win the next election?

NELLA. Will we win? With conditions the way they are? I ask you.

MIMSY. She asked you first.

NELLA. (*Rises, crosses Up Left.*) We can't lose, Miss Van der Wyck. So let's get to important matters. After we win, what do you want? Ambassador to Brazil, Senator from Maine? I'm picking jobs I know the ladies like.

AUNT HETTIE. I want nothing, Mr. Nella, except better government. Of course, I would be pleased if something could be done about taxes.

NELLA. Miss Van der Wyck, in our platform for the next election we are going to promise the American people an entirely new tax structure.

AUNT HETTIE. Really, Mr. Nella?

NELLA. For chairman of the board, presidents of corporations, and officers of unions, taxes will go down. (*Crosses to Right Center.*) For voters on relief, political appointees, and majority stockholders, taxes will also go down. But for everyone in the middle—well, they're working so hard to pay last year's taxes they won't notice how we're going to sock 'em on next year's taxes!

AUNT HETTIE. But, Mr. Nella, you promised.

NELLA. Promises and batting averages are made to be broken.

AUNT HETTIE. I see.

NELLA. I want you to be a practical politician.

AUNT HETTIE. (*Rises, crosses to 509 door.*) It must

be one of the most embarrassing experiences in the world, Mr. Nella, for a mother to see her son grow up to be a politician. And as for giving you my support, sir, I wouldn't vote for you if you were running for your life, and you better start now! (*She opens the door.* NELLA *exits to hall.*)

NELLA. And you expect us to cut your taxes! (*He exits, goes downstairs.*)

AUNT HETTIE. Well. Let's never mention him again. Nor politics either. The way politicians go after your money, you'd think they were your relatives, and the moment a person *does* come into a little money—

MIMSY. I thought we're getting lots of money.

AUNT HETTIE. We are, but don't interrupt, dear.

PUSEY. Well, you know what Hamilton said about money.

MIMSY. Don't interrupt, dear. Oh! Professor Pusey! I'm terribly sorry. I didn't mean to say "dear." Oh, dear I— I'd better tidy up the bedroom. Excuse me, please. (*She races into the bedroom.*)

AUNT HETTIE. Such a precious child, don't you think, Professor?

PUSEY. Oh, yes.

AUNT HETTIE. They don't make girls like that any more.

PUSEY. I wonder why?

AUNT HETTIE. Of course, she did leave me here to put aside the breakfast things.

PUSEY. Why don't you go in and help your niece, Miss Van der Wyck? I'll straighten this room. I'll just take this apron and the duster— (*From chair Left of sideboard.*)

AUNT HETTIE. You? Dust? Why, I've never heard of a man being asked to do such a thing!

PUSEY. You probably haven't known many men.

AUNT HETTIE. Don't you believe it.

PUSEY. (*Stacking dishes on tray.*) There were beaux in the old days?

AUNT HETTIE. Scads of them.

PUSEY. And you never considered marriage?

AUNT HETTIE. The ones with money were generally weak. And the ones without were generally looking for it. However, there was one beau who was an exception. Langley was his name. Langley Collyer. Nothing ever came of it. He was a bit on the adventurous side. Well— I'll go help our Mimsy. (*She exits into bedroom.*)

(PUSEY *puts on apron, starts to dust. The elevator door opens. A wet-nosed, in-bred young man who, only God knows how, got through the Harvard Law School, emerges. This is* AUBREY MCKITTRIDGE. *He carries a large box of candy, a larger box of flowers, a bulging briefcase. He thanks* OLD JIM.)

MCKITTRIDGE. Thank you. (*The elevator descends.* MCKITTRIDGE *juggles his packages, knocks smartly on the door.*) Aubrey McKittridge here! (*Startled,* PUSEY *opens door.*) Ah, you must be Mimsy.

PUSEY. No. I'm Pusey.

AUNT HETTIE. (*Enters from the bedroom.*) Who's there, Professor?

MCKITTRIDGE. (*He enters room.*) Good morning. I am Mr. McKittridge. You must be the lovely Mimsy Van der Wyck.

AUNT HETTIE. Don't be a fool, sir. I'm no more Mimsy than you are Rollo McKittridge. He was my age.

MIMSY. (*Enters.*) I'm Mimsy.

MCKITTRIDGE. I'm Aubrey, Rollo's son. I inherited the case from my father.

AUNT HETTIE. When did he pass away?

MCKITTRIDGE. Oh, he's not dead. He's retired. But here I stand gawking before the two most famous ladies in New York City today. Miss Van der Wyck, this is for you. (*He hands candy to* MIMSY.)

MIMSY. Oh, thank you.

MCKITTRIDGE. And, Miss Van der Wyck, these are

for you. I do hope they'll please you. (*He hands flowers to* AUNT HETTIE.)

AUNT HETTIE. They are lovely, and I thank you, Mr. McKittridge. Mimsy, do put them in a vase, please.

MIMSY. Yes, Aunt Hettie. (*And she promptly does so, popping them in vase on sideboard.*) There we are.

McKITTRIDGE. I say, aren't you going to put a drop of water in that vase?

MIMSY. Oh, we put water in the vases this morning.

McKITTRIDGE. You did?

AUNT HETTIE. The landlord wants to turn it off; the water and the electricity and everything else. But now that our attorney is here, he'll take care of everything, won't you, Mr. McKittridge?

McKITTRIDGE. Miss Van der Wyck, I don't want you to fret about a thing. You're in good hands again.

AUNT HETTIE. It's nice to hear that, sir.

McKITTRIDGE. As you say, I'll take care of everything. Early next week I'll send one of our junior partners up here and you can explain matters to him.

MIMSY. (*Right of table.*) But they're going to turn off the water today.

AUNT HETTIE. In two hours they're going to turn it off!

McKITTRIDGE. Now, I don't want you to worry about a thing. I've already solved your little problem. Undoubtedly, your landlord would be susceptible to certain kinds of pressure. Notice how we lawyers think?

AUNT HETTIE. Not yet, I haven't.

McKITTRIDGE. (*Back of table.*) But you will, you will, you will! As I was stepping into the elevator downstairs just now I saw a gentleman to whom our firm has made contributions year after year. And Francis X. Nella won't be the man to refuse us a favor.

AUNT HETTIE. You gave money to the Democratic Party?

McKITTRIDGE. We give money to both parties. It's what we in the law call "playing it safe." But enough!

Anything that our firm can do to make you happy and comfortable—we'll move heaven and earth to do it.

AUNT HETTIE. (*Rising, crosses to whatnot Down Left.*) Those are welcome words, Mr. McKittridge. And if you don't mind, we're going to take advantage of them. Right now. We have these bills.

McKITTRIDGE. Bills? You mean currency? Cash?

AUNT HETTIE. No. I mean bills as in rent. We've done nothing about it for eight months.

McKITTRIDGE. Eight months! Naughty, naughty, naughty. Why not, Miss Van der Wyck?

AUNT HETTIE. No, no, no money, Mr. McKittridge.

McKITTRIDGE. Oh. Well, what happened to it?

MIMSY. (*Sits Right of table.*) That's what *you* are going to tell *us*.

AUNT HETTIE. That's why you're here.

McKITTRIDGE. Well, I— I didn't come for that exact reason. I was under the impression that you and your niece still had uh—

AUNT HETTIE. What?

McKITTRIDGE. Well, our records show that certain securities and the—uh—world-famous Van der Wyck collection of diamonds, and a rather substantial amount of cash are still in your possession, and I thought if I could be of any further service to you—

MIMSY. All of that is gone.

McKITTRIDGE. Gone?! (*He forces a laugh.*) How amusing. (*Straight to* AUNT HETTIE.) What does she mean "gone"?

AUNT HETTIE. As in going, going. But that inheritance from my brother, Rensselaer. That didn't go under during the Depression, did it?

McKITTRIDGE. Not at all.

MIMSY. Would it be all right if you told us about it?

AUNT HETTIE. Yes. Wouldn't you like to sit down, Mr. McKittridge?

McKITTRIDGE. Thank you.

AUNT HETTIE. Professor Pusey, there. (*Indicating window seat.*)

PUSEY. Thank you.

MIMSY. (*Stopping* PUSEY *as he starts to move.*) Adam is doing very well as he is, Aunt Hettie.

AUNT HETTIE. As you say, dear. Now then, Mr. McKittridge. We're ready.

McKITTRIDGE. For what?

AUNT HETTIE. A financial report on our holdings.

McKITTRIDGE. A financial report? Certainly. What would you like to hear?

MIMSY. What about air conditioners?

AUNT HETTIE. The patent on air conditioning? How is it making out?

McKITTRIDGE. The basic elements of refrigeration employed by every manufacturer are still controlled by that patent.

MIMSY. And nylon. How's business with nylon?

McKITTRIDGE. It's the biggest thing of its kind on the world market today.

AUNT HETTIE. And Mimsy and I own it.

McKITTRIDGE. Not any more you don't. Now, now, now, no need to frown, Miss Van der Wyck. You didn't lose the patents. We sold them.

AUNT HETTIE. You sold them? Who gave you permission? And for how much?

McKITTRIDGE. Well, it's difficult to give a precise figure at this date, but roughly—one hundred and seventy million dollars.

AUNT HETTIE. One hundred and seventy million? That seems a satisfactory figure. Not too high, not too low. When did you make the sale?

McKITTRIDGE. Well, after you'd been gone for ten years, the courts had to rule on whether you were alive or dead. They decided you were—dead.

AUNT HETTIE. Typical of the law—jumping to conclusions.

McKITTRIDGE. Two days later, we arranged for your memorial service at St. Paul's.

MIMSY. That was nice.

AUNT HETTIE. Who was there?

McKITTRIDGE. No one. However, you weren't entirely forgotten. The day your will was put into probate, twenty-two hundred relatives stormed the courthouse.

AUNT HETTIE. Such effrontery! Mimsy and I have no relatives!

McKITTRIDGE. There were law suits attempting to prove otherwise.

AUNT HETTIE. Don't tell me you allowed those impostors to get away with anything?

McKITTRIDGE. My dear Miss Van der Wyck. Three and a half years of pre-law at Harvard. Four years of the Harvard Law School. Two and a half years of graduate study in wills, trusts, and patents. I have devoted my entire life to protecting the money which forms the bulk of your estate.

AUNT HETTIE. May heaven bless you, Mr. McKittridge. You and your dear father. I can't express my gratitude for such loyalty and devotion.

McKITTRIDGE. Thank you for those kind words, Miss Van der Wyck. I feel rewarded already for the entire struggle. And I know Daddy will when I write him of our meeting. You know, Daddy became ill after the fifth year of litigation. That's when we bought the island.

MIMSY. An island? You bought an island?

McKITTRIDGE. We bought it for you.

AUNT HETTIE. If we were dead, why did we need an island?

McKITTRIDGE. To save you money, rather than charge you the usual fee for sending our people on holidays. You see, our family worked so hard to keep the estate from your family that there was scarcely a moment when one of us wasn't completely exhausted. So—we realized it would be cheaper for you if we bought a small island near Nassau and had you put up a shack.

AUNT HETTIE. How big a shack? How many rooms?

McKITTRIDGE. Daddy's, Uncle Henry's, or mine? But let's not linger over details. You *should* know that for a period of eighteen months one of the lower courts ruled in favor of giving the entire estate to your alleged relatives. But we fought them tooth and nail. We beat them, but, oh, the money it cost you.

AUNT HETTIE. How much?

McKITTRIDGE. Well, there were the claimants and their attorneys, and witnesses and their attorneys; quite often there were attorneys for the attorneys.

MIMSY. Well, at least we *do* have the hundred and seventy million.

McKITTRIDGE. Oh, I wish we did. You see, there were taxes to be paid during all these years.

AUNT HETTIE. How much were they?

McKITTRIDGE. One hundred million.

AUNT HETTIE. A hundred million in taxes! I would have let them lock me up before I'd pay it.

McKITTRIDGE. Apparently you don't mind being locked up, but Daddy and I do. We paid!

MIMSY. Then give us what's left.

McKITTRIDGE. Well, I'm sorry to say, there were other expenses, too.

AUNT HETTIE. Such as?

McKITTRIDGE. Legal fees. You see, once we got hold of this case, we practically gave up every other client we represented.

MIMSY. What's left *after* legal fees?

McKITTRIDGE. I'm coming to that. But you must understand there were court costs, executor's fees, records of proceedings.

MIMSY. I understand, but how much have we got?

McKITTRIDGE. I'm coming to that, too. Then there are certified vouchers for identification of witnesses.

MIMSY. Anything else?

McKITTRIDGE. Yes. Transportation and travel.

MIMSY. Well, how much is left?

McKITTRIDGE. And then there were fountain pens, pencils, pen wipers—

AUNT HETTIE. Mr. McKittridge!

McKITTRIDGE. Rubber bands, ink, paper clips. Oh, it's amazing how these things add up.

AUNT HETTIE. I am prepared to be amazed. As of this morning, what've we got left in the bank?

McKITTRIDGE. I'm glad you asked that question. (*Picking up statement.*) $3,121.00.

AUNT HETTIE. Three thousand dollars!

MIMSY. And a beautiful island.

McKITTRIDGE. Unfortunately, we had to sell the island a few years ago. You were short of funds.

AUNT HETTIE. You and Daddy and the rest of the family were not?

McKITTRIDGE. Hardly. We bought it. Tut, tut, tut. No need to frown.

PUSEY. Yes, you do have *some* money. Enough to see you through your current problems.

AUNT HETTIE. Don't be so certain. May we have a check for three thousand dollars, Mr. McKittridge?

McKITTRIDGE. I don't know quite how to say this.

AUNT HETTIE. Try. Let one little word lead to another.

McKITTRIDGE. Your legal bill for this fiscal year, Miss Van der Wyck, it hasn't been paid.

AUNT HETTIE. I'm not going to ask how much. You'll tell me soon enough.

McKITTRIDGE. Yes. It's twenty-five thousand. And that, minus thirty-one twenty-one means that all you owe us is $21,779.

AUNT HETTIE. (*Crosses Up to sideboard.*) We owe you? Mimsy, fix this phone. Call Chicago. I'm going to get Clarence Darrow!

(OLD JIM *and* MISS FREUD *emerge from elevator.*)

OLD JIM. I thought you civil service workers weren't influenced by politicians. (*Knocks.*) It's Old Jim. And Old Miss Freud.

AUNT HETTIE. (*Opens door.*) Come in!

MISS FREUD. Greetings from your New York City Welfare Department.

OLD JIM. Greetings from your Western Union, Professor. (*He hands* PUSEY *a telegram.*)

MISS FREUD. This is urgent. May I speak with you ladies? This is urgent.

MIMSY. Roger.

PUSEY. (*Sits chair Right.*) Oh, my goodness!

MIMSY. What is it, Professor?

PUSEY. I've been dropped from the faculty.

MIMSY. By whom?

PUSEY. The Dean of the "Jay" School. He read in the paper that I was spending the night in a hotel room with two New York women. He says "When I suggested you go to the big City to pick up some experience, I didn't mean that kind."

MIMSY. Oh, Professor.

MISS FREUD. Let's get on with our business. His being fired is no concern of mine. He's not a resident of the City of New York. Ladies, your Welfare Department has just ruled that this building is unsafe for habitation.

AUNT HETTIE. But you said you'd help us stay here.

MISS FREUD. I said that yesterday. Today, I'm saying something else.

AUNT HETTIE. Well, at least you're not stubborn.

MISS FREUD. Furthermore, your Department has also ruled, quote "Anyone who chooses to remain locked up in a room for twenty-six years may not be considered a properly adjusted adult human being."

AUNT HETTIE. (*Crosses to* Down Left.*) Well, I'll be damned! What do you expect us to do?

MISS FREUD. It's too late for *you* to do anything.

MIMSY. Miss Freud, we've been staying here just because we like it. But if you think— I mean, we're perfectly willing to do whatever you think is best, if only—

MISS FREUD. Evidently, you do not understand governmental efficiency. Cooperation will get you nowhere. Both of you are being remanded at once to Welfare Island.

AUNT HETTIE. Welfare Island! I'll not go to such a place.

MISS FREUD. (*Crosses to her.*) Under the "B" clause of Section Six you have no alternative. Of course, if people in *your* position don't wish to take advantage of your City's facilities, you can enter any of the *private* institutions. Sunshine Rock, for instance.

McKITTRIDGE. Sunshine Rock? Cousin Eric has been there for sixteen years. That's the most expensive sanitarium in the state.

AUNT HETTIE. Sanitarium? How dare you suggest we go to a sanitarium?

McKITTRIDGE. Yes. They haven't got a dime.

MISS FREUD. But this morning's Times said they owned—

McKITTRIDGE. They did, but now they don't.

AUNT HETTIE. And he ought to know because now he does.

MISS FREUD. (*Crosses back to Center.*) No money! Why, this makes it an open and shut case. You need help and I'm really going to give it to you. It's Welfare Island for you—(*To* AUNT HETTIE.) and City Relief for you. (*To* MIMSY.)

MIMSY. (*Crosses to* AUNT HETTIE.) Aunt Hettie, stop them.

MISS FREUD. I'll be back at noon. Commitment papers, attendants, and duplicate W6K-101 forms. Miss Van der Wyck, I'm sorry to have had to do this, but if I didn't, tomorrow I'd be assigned to unmarried mothers in Far Rockaway. (*She exits.*)

MIMSY. (*Crosses to him.*) Mr. McKittridge, can't you do anything?

McKITTRIDGE. I?— I'm already late for court as it is.

PUSEY. Won't you do something to help them?

McKITTRIDGE. Oh, I couldn't. The Van der Wycks have their motto. We have ours. Cum navis obruitur, desere. (*He exits into hall.*)

OLD JIM. (*Follows him.*) Say, what does that motto of yours mean?

McKITTRIDGE. It's Latin.

OLD JIM. Yes, but what does it say?

McKITTRIDGE. When the ship is sinking, desert!

(*They go down in elevator.*)

PUSEY. Well—what are you going to do?

AUNT HETTIE. I don't know. Not yet.

MIMSY. (*Crosses to her; they embrace.*) Aunt Hettie, I'm afraid. I've never been away from you for a single night of my life.

PUSEY. Miss Van der Wyck? Mimsy? If there's anything *I* can do— I mean, if you'd like to stay in my hotel room—

MIMSY. (*Whirling on him.*) You? You just got fired for associating with the wrong kind of women! How do you expect me to trust you? (*Fresh tears.*)

AUNT HETTIE. Now, now, Mimsy.

MIMSY. Well, I'm scared!

AUNT HETTIE. You must grow up, Mimsy. You must learn to lead a new kind of life.

MIMSY. No, no, Aunt Hettie, I don't want to leave you.

AUNT HETTIE. Stop it! Stop it, Mimsy! Dry your eyes, dab your nose, and go on to the next thing! Do you hear me?

MIMSY. (*Taken aback.*) Yes, Aunt Hettie. Why— you've never spoken to me like that.

AUNT HETTIE. I've done very little for you, Mimsy, and I have very little to leave you, but I *can* teach you how to face adversity! Now, what is the next thing?

MIMSY. We'd better pack.

AUNT HETTIE. A splendid beginning, dear. Very well. Professor, will you be good enough to help us pack? There are some old suitcases in that closet in the bedroom. (PUSEY *exits.*) Now, Mimsy, where do we begin?

MIMSY. Well, we're not going to leave the things I worked on, Aunt Hettie.

AUNT HETTIE. All of your arts and crafts, dear?

MIMSY. The butterfly collection. That's valuable.

AUNT HETTIE. That's on loan with Mr. Lefkowitz, dear. Remember?

(PUSEY *re-enters with suitcases.*)

MIMSY. Oh, yes. Well, what about my tapestry?

AUNT HETTIE. Mimsy, it's so big and it isn't quite finished.

MIMSY. I worked three whole years on that tapestry while you read me the complete Diary of Samuel Pepys, and I'm not going to leave Samuel Pepys and the Rhine Maidens behind.

PUSEY. (*Pointing to tapestry.*) Oh. Is that who they are? The Rhine Maidens?

MIMSY. Do you like it, Professor?

PUSEY. Oh, very much.

MIMSY. That settles it. We're taking the tapestry, Aunt Hettie.

PUSEY. Do you want me to get it down?

AUNT HETTIE. No, thank you, Professor. Mimsy and I took it down every day when she worked on it. We have a system. But you *could* get us some twine to tie it up with. I believe it's in that corner cupboard there. Are you ready, Mimsy?

MIMSY. In a moment.

(*The* TWO LADIES, *standing on chairs, start to untie the top of the tapestry from the brass rod which holds it up.* PUSEY *is searching for the twine in whatnot.*)

AUNT HETTIE. Have you found the twine, Professor? (PUSEY *has found the stock certificate.*) I say, have you found the twine?

PUSEY. Where'd you get this?

AUNT HETTIE. What?

PUSEY. This.

AUNT HETTIE. Oh, that's a share of some stock we once had.

PUSEY. Not one share. It says here 500 shares.

AUNT HETTIE. That's right. That's what they all said. Five hundred shares. They're worthless. Ready, Mimsy?

PUSEY. Do you have any more?

AUNT HETTIE. No, we don't have any more.

MIMSY. A long time ago, when the landlord wouldn't redecorate, I papered the wall with it.

PUSEY. You papered the wall with General Motors stock?

AUNT HETTIE. All set, Mimsy?

MIMSY. Let go!

(They drop the tapestry to the floor. From the floor to the ceiling, the wall is covered with large white certificates, edged in green, and stamped in gold. PUSEY, however, is burrowing in the top drawer.)

AUNT HETTIE. Whatever are you looking for, Professor?

PUSEY. *(Faces them.)* I just want to make sure there aren't one or two of these left.

(He buries his face in the drawer again, and then comes out. A leap to the wall, and he is stripping off a loose certificate. AUNT HETTIE removes a panel of photographs of Republican Presidents. Guess what's glued to the wall behind those old boys? You're right.)

CURTAIN

ACT TWO

SCENE 3

SCENE: *The same, evening.*

AT RISE: *And how things have changed! The back wall of the sitting room has been stripped clean, show-*

*ing bare plaster and an occasional section of wooden
slats behind the plaster. The mantel is clear and
most of the furniture is gone. Doors yawn open to
reveal empty closets. However, a shiny new ward-
robe trunk and an elegant set of matched luggage
may be seen. Seated on the edge of the armchair,
wretched and uncomfortable, is* AUBREY MCKITT-
RIDGE. *Before him stands a snappy and confident*
PROFESSOR PUSEY.

PUSEY. During the years I was working on my Master's degree— (*Christmas tree LIGHTS blink.*) Excuse
me. That's the telephone again. It hasn't stopped ringing,
all afternoon, all evening, the telephone.

MCKITTRIDGE. Are you sure—?

PUSEY. (*Holding up finger for quiet.*) Would you
mind, please? (MCKITTRIDGE, *who opened his mouth to
speak, closes it.*) Five-oh-nine. No, they aren't— No,
I'm sorry, but they are not accepting any dinner invita-
tions, Mr. Baruch— This is Professor Pusey, their business manager— Well, I was fired from the University
and it's either working for the Van der Wycks or join-
ing the Franciscan Brothers. And I've never liked getting
up early in the morning— Not at all. Goodbye. (*He
hangs up.*) Now, as I was saying, during the years I was
working on my Master's degree—

MCKITTRIDGE. It is not, Professor, that I am bored
listening to the story of your life. Certainly not. But
are you sure I can't see Miss Van der Wyck yet?

PUSEY. I've told you, Mr. McKittridge, they're still
dressing.

MCKITTRIDGE. Are you certain the city psychiatrist
gave them a clean bill of health?

PUSEY. Oh, yes. He said that the way world conditions
have been for the last twenty-six years, the Van der
Wycks weren't crazy for staying *in*. It's the people who
are *out* that need help.

MCKITTRIDGE. Shocking! Shocking!

(*Elevator arrives. Entire* PRESS CORPS *pours out.* OLD
JIM *knocks at the door to 509.*)

OLD JIM. It's Old Jim!

(PUSEY *opens the door.*)

RYAN. Let us in, Professor!

(*They push their way in.*)

ROSENTHAL. What kind of bagels can you get from a
hock shop?

PUSEY. Quiet please! I did not allow noisy students,
I will not allow a noisy press.

OLD JIM. (*Handing bag to* PUSEY.) From the Lefkowitz Loan Company.

PUSEY. (*Starts to bedroom door with bag.*) Thank
you, Jim. Miss Van der Wyck, James has just come back
from the Lefkowitz Loan Company.

(MIMSY's *hand appears, takes bag.*)

MIMSY's VOICE. Thank you, Professor. Here they are,
Aunt Hettie.

AUNT HETTIE. Thank you.

MIMSY's VOICE. Aunt Hettie says to thank you, too,
James.

OLD JIM. Not at all, glad to be of help. Better tell
'em the car's downstairs.

PUSEY. (*Knocks on door.*) Miss Van der Wyck, your
car and chauffeur are waiting.

AUNT HETTIE's VOICE. Thank you, Professor.

OLD JIM. Will you be long? The cop on the beat had
to call for extra men. All those people and television
cameras in the street.

AUNT HETTIE's VOICE. We shan't be long, James.
Come along, Mimsy. Don't dawdle, child.

MIMSY's VOICE. I'm ready, Aunt Hettie. Are you?

AUNT HETTIE'S VOICE. Me? I'm ready for anything.

(Arm in arm, AUNT HETTIE *and* MIMSY *enter Down Left Center. They now wear ermine wraps, jeweled necklaces, bracelets. even a diamond tiara.)*

RYAN. Hold it!

MCKITTRIDGE. Oh, Miss Van der Wyck.

ROSENTHAL. How does it feel to be out?

JOHNSON. Who will you support for President?

SUMMERS. What about foreign policy?

RYAN. Miss Van der Wyck, are you Republicans now or Democrats?

AUNT HETTIE. Neither.

RYAN. You're against both?

AUNT HETTIE. No, sir. We are *for* both parties. And for no other party. We are merely opposed to those few professional politicians who get their hooks into the public office and keep them there.

ROSENTHAL. What're you going to do with the dough?

AUNT HETTIE. Well, since one political party is composed of liberal conservatives, and the other of conservative liberals, my niece and I are going to endow a few universities with chairs of political science. The voters should be able to tell one party from the other.

MCKITTRIDGE. Please, Miss Van der Wyck!

RYAN. What about your personal lives?

JOHNSON. What're you going to do now that you've come out?

MIMSY. We're going right back in again.

AUNT HETTIE. This afternoon we bought three floors in the Waldorf Towers. My niece, Professor Pusey, and I are going to take one apiece. James will accompany us.

OLD JIM. They're giving me more than Equity minimum.

MCKITTRIDGE. Miss Van der Wyck—

AUNT HETTIE. Leaving for court, Mr. McKittridge?

MCKITTRIDGE. Oh, no. I'm completely at your service, my dear ladies, completely devoted to your interests.

AUNT HETTIE. Well, that's more than I am to yours. What do you want?

McKITTRIDGE. That General Motors stock—

AUNT HETTIE. That's what I thought you wanted.

McKITTRIDGE. No, no, no, you misunderstand. I'm here to protect that little nest egg of yours.

AUNT HETTIE. Little! We peeled 30,000 shares off those walls.

PUSEY. And those were the original shares, Mr. McKittridge. Since then, General Motors has been split eight times.

MIMSY. (*She opens box.*) Would you mind, Professor? In the good old days when we went out in the evening, the ladies wore furs and dinner gowns. And the gentlemen wore opera capes and silk hats. (*She snaps open opera hat, offers,* PUSEY *puts on cape.*) And now, Professor, dear, if—you—please. (MIMSY *takes one arm,* AUNT HETTIE, *the other.*)

AUNT HETTIE. May we, Professor?

McKITTRIDGE. Miss Van der Wyck, if I could just have a word.

AUNT HETTIE. Why, of course, Mr. McKittridge. Why don't you give us a call next week. We won't be home to you, but keep trying. (*She turns away.*)

McKITTRIDGE. (*He takes* MIMSY *aside, steps on trap plate.*) Miss Van der Wyck, if I am ever in a position to please you—

MIMSY. Oh, you're in the perfect position right now!

(*She races to the switch and throws it. The net drops.* PUSEY *offers his arm to* MIMSY, *to* AUNT HETTIE, *and triumphantly they exit.*)

THE CURTAIN FALLS

THE GIRLS IN 509

PROPERTY PLOT

Pay dial phone on wall in hall.

Small bench Down Right of elevator Right.

2 radiators—one at room division—one under window seat Down Left.

Umbrella stand Down Right of first radiator.

Chair above stand.

Temperature chart and graph w/pencil on red ribbon hangs on onstage side of 509 door.

Fireplace, andirons up of 509 door w/dressing.

Doorstop.

Table Up Right Center; on it picture Wm. McKinley in silver frame, lamp, dressing.

Pictures of Republican Presidents on wall Up Right.

Tapestry on wall Up Center, which covers stock certificates.

Large sideboard in front of tapestry; on it old-fashioned phone w/long cord, vases, gloves (MIMSY) and under it a crystal punch bowl.

Chair Right and Left of sideboard.

Cupboard whatnot Left of bedroom door; on it matches in dish, ashtray, cigarette holders and cigarettes—second shelf, books, political pamphlet.

In drawer, stock certificate and stack of bills.

Window seat Down Left.

Table Left Center: armchair Left—small chair above—and, at rise, matching chair in front of fireplace.

Extra dressing: plastocene head (sideboard) w/stuffed bird on top. Electric fan Upstage end of fireplace mantel. Stuffed squirrel on bird's-eye lamp. Small hassock Down Left.

Trap lid leaning against sideboard—Small circular rug, covering trap plate, Center.

ACT ONE—Scene 1

Off Right:

Service cart w/breakfast set for two.
Letter (OLD JIM).
$5 bill (RYAN).
Briefcase w/papers, spring pencil (FREUD).
Copypaper and pencil (PUSEY).
Camera w/flash attachments (RYAN).
Copypaper and pencils (REPORTERS).
Bucket, rags, mop, sweeper (OLD JIM).

Off Left:

Spectacles (AUNT HETTIE).
2 books (AUNT HETTIE—MIMSY).
Exercise chart (MIMSY).
Alarm clock (practical).
2 suitcases (PUSEY II-2).
Dressing rooms.

ACT ONE—Scene 2

Trap down to one-half.
D-switch open.
Move cart Up Center.
Place ashtray on table Left Center.
Move chair from front of fireplace to Right of table.
Tie PUSEY in chair Right w/women's stockings, sheet,
    handkerchief, curtain cord w/tassel.

Off Left:

Tray w/ champagne bottle (open) and three glasses
    (MIMSY).

ACT TWO—Scene 1

Trap down one-fourth.
Strike cart.
Hat on table Left Center (ALLEN).
Glass of water on table.
AUNT HETTIE's spectacles on whatnot.
Circular rug back—trap lid ajar.
D-switch out.

Off Left:
Goggles (MIMSY).

ACT TWO—SCENE 2

Set firebell wires.
509 door unlocked.
Window seat cushion, sheet, pillow, blanket at fireplace.
Breakfast for three at table Left Center.
Cart at table w/half full glass of water.
Move phone to sideboard.
N. Y. Times on table Left Center.
Duster and apron (PUSEY) on sideboard.
Off Right:
Telegram (OLD JIM).
Flowers wrapped in paper, box of candy, briefcase
w/papers (MCKITTRIDGE).
Off Left:
Tool belt and tools (MIMSY).
Christmas tree lights on rolling pin (MIMSY).
2 suitcases (PUSEY).

ACT TWO—SCENE 3

2 new panels in.
Strike cart.
Strike table Left Center and two small chairs.
Move armchair to mark.
Place suitcase right of armchair w/phone on it.
Place box containing opera cape and hat for PUSEY on
window seat Down Left.
D-switch out.
Off Right:
Large paper bag (OLD JIM).

HERE'S HOW

A Basic Stagecraft Book

THOROUGHLY REVISED
AND ENLARGED

by HERBERT V. HAKE

COVERING 59 topics on the essentials of stagecraft (13 of them brand new). *Here's How* meets a very real need in the educational theater. It gives to directors and others concerned with the technical aspects of play production a complete and graphic explanation of ways of handling fundamental stagecraft problems.

The book is exceptional on several counts. It not only treats every topic thoroughly, but does so in an easy-to-read style every layman can understand. Most important, it is prepared in such a way that for every topic there is a facing page of illustrations (original drawings and photographs)—thus giving the reader a complete graphic presentation of the topic along with the textual description of the topic.

Because of the large type, the large size of the pages (9″ x 12″), and the flexible metal binding, *Here's How* will lie flat when opened and can be laid on a workbench for a director to read while in a *standing* position.

Price, $4.50 postpaid

#104

LADY PRECIOUS STREAM

Chinese play. 4 acts. By S. I. Hsiung. 5 males, 5 females (extras). Conventional Chinese scene for all sets. Chinese costumes.

This Chinese play by S. I. Hsiung was produced successfully in New York and in London, where it was performed more than 500 times. It is in every respect an authentic play written and performed in the Chinese manner with the delightful and charming conventions of that ancient institution. This beautiful romantic drama of love, fidelity, treachery and poetry is a decidedly colorful fantasy that appeals to all classes of theater goers. It tells, in varied scenes, of the devotion of a wife for her adventurous husband, of his prowess as a warrior and his ultimate return.

(Royalty, $25.00.)

CHARLEY'S AUNT

Farcical comedy. 3 acts. By Brandon Thomas. 7 males, 5 females. Interior, exterior. Modern costumes.

The first act introduces us to Jack Chesney's rooms in college. He is violently in love with Kitty Verdun. A chum of his, Charles Wykeham, is in the same quandary, loving Miss Spettigue. The young men at once lay their plans and ask the objects of their affections to join them at their rooms for luncheon—in order to meet Donna Lucia D'-Alvadorez, Charley's aunt, who is expected to arrive from Brazil. Miss Spettigue and Miss Verdun accept the invitation, but the millionaire Donna from the antipodes sends a telegram saying that she will have to defer her visit for a few days. The problem is solved at once by forcing another undergraduate of the name of Lord Fancourt Babberley into a black satin skirt, a lace fichu, a pair of mitts, an old-fashioned cap and wig. As Charley's Aunt, then, this old frump is introduced to the sweethearts, to Jack Chesney's father, and to Stephen Spettigue. Unexpectedly the real aunt turns up, but she assumes the name of Mrs. Smith or Smythe. To attain his object,—viz., the rich widow's hand— the solicitor invites everybody to dinner. She gets his consent to the marriage of his ward to young Chesney, and eventually everybody but the avaricious solicitor is rendered overwhelmingly happy.

(Royalty, $25.00.)

6

OUR TOWN

Drama. 3 acts. By Thornton Wilder. 17 males, 7
females, extras. Bare stage. Costumes, 1901.

Winner of the Pulitzer Prize, 1939. The play begins in
1901 in Grover's Corners where the Gibbs and the Webbs
are neighbors. During their childhood George Gibbs and
Emily Webb are playmates and their lives are inextricably
woven together as neighbor's lives are like to be. But as
they grow older they pass from this period into a state of
romantic but embarrassed interest in one another. And one
day, after a slight quarrel, George proposes to Emily in
the drug store over an ice cream soda. They are a fine
young couple, but their happiness is short-lived, for Emily
is taken in death and placed in the village cemetery on a
rainy, dreary day. In the most vitally moving scene in the
modern theatre is shown the peace and quiet of death which
can never be understood by the living. Emily, at first, doesn't
understand it, and not until she has gone back to relive her
twelfth birthday does she understand that life is a transient
fleeting thing and death brings an eternal peace. She takes
her place in the graveyard with her friends while George,
unable to see beyond his grief, mourns for her.

(Royalty, $50-$25.)

TEN LITTLE INDIANS

Mystery. 3 acts. By Agatha Christie. 9 males, 3
females. Interior. Modern costumes.

A superlative type of mystery comedy, first produced at
the Broadhurst Theatre in New York. The play takes place
in a weird old house on an island. In the house is a mantel-
piece on which there are ten little wooden Indians, and
above which is an inscription of the nursery rhyme, telling
how each little Indian died—until there were none. Ten
people are gathered in the house as guests of a mysterious
and unseen host. They hear the voice of the host accuse
them, each in his turn, of complicity in a murder. Then one
by one the guests suffer the different deaths predicted by
the voice, and one by one the little wooden Indians topple.
With seven down and three to go, the audience is still sus-
picious and in a fever of excitement. What follows is a
tremendously gripping finale, expertly done by one of
America's top mystery writers.

(Royalty, $50.00.)

6 RMS RIV VU
BOB RANDALL

(Little Theatre) Comedy
4 Men, 4 Women, Interior

A vacant apartment with a river view is open for inspection by prospective tenants, and among them are a man and a woman who have never met before. They are the last to leave and, when they get ready to depart, they find that the door is locked and they are shut in. Since they are attractive young people, they find each other interesting and the fact that both are happily married adds to their delight of mutual, yet obviously separate interests.

> ". . . a Broadway comedy of fun and class, as cheerful as a rising souffle. A sprightly, happy comedy of charm and humor. Two people playing out a very vital game of love, an attractive fantasy with a precious tincture of truth to it."— N.Y. *Times*. ". . . perfectly charming entertainment, sexy, romantic and funny."—*Women's Wear Daily*.

Royalty, $50–$35

WHO KILLED SANTA CLAUS?
TERENCE FEELY

(All Groups) Thriller
6 Men, 2 Women, Interior

Barbara Love is a popular television 'auntie'. It is Christmas, and a number of men connected with her are coming to a party. Her secretary, Connie, is also there. Before they arrive she is threatened by a disguised voice on her Ansaphone, and is sent a grotesque 'murdered' doll in a coffin, wearing a dress resembling one of her own. She calls the police, and a handsome detective arrives. Shortly afterwards her guests follow. It becomes apparent that one of those guests is planning to kill her. Or is it the strange young man who turns up unexpectedly, claiming to belong to the publicity department, but unknown to any of the others?

> ". . . is a thriller with heaps of suspense, surprises, and nattily cleaver turns and twists . . . Mr. Feeley is technically highly skilled in the artificial range of operations, and his dialogue is brilliantly effective."—The Stage. London.

Royalty, $50–$25

THE SEA HORSE
EDWARD J. MOORE

(Little Theatre) Drama
I Man, I Woman, Interior

It is a play that is, by turns, tender, ribald, funny and suspenseful.
Audiences everywhere will take it to their hearts because it is
touched with humanity and illuminates with glowing sympathy the
complexities of a man-woman relationship. Set in a West Coast
waterfront bar, the play is about Harry Bales, a seaman, who, when
on shore leave, usually heads for "The Sea Horse," the bar run by
Gertrude Blum, the heavy, unsentimental proprietor. Their relationship
is purely physical and, as the play begins, they have never confided
their private yearnings to each other. But this time Harry has returned
with a dream: to buy a charter fishing boat and to have a son by
Gertrude. She, in her turn, has made her life one of hard work, by
day, and nocturnal love-making; she has encased her heart behind a
facade of toughness, utterly devoid of sentimentality, because of a
failed marriage. Irwin's play consists in the ritual of "dance" court-
ship by Harry of Gertrude, as these two outwardly abrasive characters
fight, make up, fight again, spin dreams, deflate them, make love and
reveal their long locked-up secrets.

"A burst of brilliance!"—*N.Y. Post.* "I was touched close to
tears!"—*Village Voice.* "A must! An incredible love story. A
beautiful play!"—*Newhouse Newspapers.* "A major new playwright!"—*Variety.*
Copies late fall. ROYALTY, $50–$35

THE AU PAIR MAN
HUGH LEONARD

(Little Theatre) Comedy
I Man, I Woman, Interior

The play concerns a rough Irish bill collector named Hartigan, who becomes a love slave and companion to an English lady named Eliza-
beth, who lives in a cluttered London town house, which looks more
like a museum for a British Empire on which the sun has long set.
Even the door bell chimes out the national anthem. Hartigan is immediately conscripted into her service in return for which she agrees
to teach him how to be a gentleman rather after the fashion of a
reverse Pygmalion. The play is a wild one, and is really the never-
ending battle between England and Ireland. Produced to critical ac-
claim at Lincoln Center's Vivian Beaumont Theatre.

ROYALTY, $50–$35

A Breeze from The Gulf

MART CROWLEY

(Little Theatre) Drama

The author of "The Boys in the Band" takes us on a journey back to a small Mississippi town to watch a 15-year-old boy suffer through adolescence to adulthood and success as a writer. His mother is a frilly southern doll who has nothing to fall back on when her beauty fades. She develops headaches and other physical problems, while the asthmatic son turns to dolls and toys at an age when other boys are turning to sports. The traveling father becomes withdrawn, takes to drink; and mother takes to drugs to kill the pain of the remembrances of things past. She eventually ends in an asylum, and the father in his fumbling way tries to tell the son to live the life he must.

> "The boy is plunged into a world of suffering he didn't create.
> . . . One of the most electrifying plays I've seen in the past few
> years . . . Scenes boil and hiss . . . The dialogue goes straight
> to the heart." Reed, Sunday News.

Royalty, $50–$35

ECHOES

N. RICHARD NASH

(All Groups) Drama

2 Men, 1 Woman, Interior

A young man and woman build a low-keyed paradise of happiness within an asylum, only to have it shattered by the intrusion of the outside world. The two characters search, at times agonizingly to determine the difference between illusion and reality. The effort is lightened at times by moments of shared love and "pretend" games, like decorating Christmas trees that are not really there. The theme of love, vulnerable to the surveillances of the asylum, and the ministrations of the psychiatrist, (a non-speaking part) seems as fragile in the constrained setting as it often is in the outside world.

> ". . . even with the tragic, sombre theme there is a note of hope
> and possible release and the situations presented specifically also
> have universal applications to give it strong effect . . . intellectual,
> but charged with emotion."—**Reed.**

Royalty, $50–$35